DELIGHTFUL
Vietnamese
COOKING

by Eng Tie Ang

AMBROSIA PUBLICATIONS

Seattle, Washington

Ambrosia Publications
P.O. Box 30818
Seattle, WA 98103
Phone (206) 789-3693
Fax   (206) 789-3693

Art Direction by: Eng Tie Ang
Cover Design by: Kate Rose
Cover Production by: Shawn Wheeler
Cover Photo by: Terry Pagos Photography
Design and Illustrations by: Eng Tie Ang
Food Styling by: Veleda Furtado and Joan Deccio Wickham
Food Styling Assistance by: Eng Tie Ang and Carla Ferreira
Editorial Direction by: Donald R. Bissonnette
Typography and Production by: Janusz Mydlarczyk
Published by: Ambrosia Publications - Seattle, Washington
Printed by: Publishers Press - Salt Lake City, Utah

Printed in the United States of America
First Edition
First Printing - 1996

ISBN: 0-9627810-3-7
Library of Congress Catalog Number: 96-85053

Dedication

    With love, thanks, and affection, I dedicate this book to my husband, Donald R. Bissonnette, for all his help and support of me over the years in my efforts to become a successful author.

On The Cover

1. Vietnamese Custard, page 140
2. Savory Fish Sauce, page 18
3. Peanut Sauce, page 17
4. Beef Lemon Grass Satay, page 24
5. Spring Rolls, page 31
6. Chicken Curry, page 120
7. Vietnamese Coffee, page 141
8. Vietnamese Chicken Salad, page 59

Table of Contents

Acknowledgements

I would like to thank many people for their help, support, and encouragement in putting this book together. First, I would like to thank those who helped in the editing process: Debbie Turner, Sara Baldwin, and my husband, Donald Richard Bissonnette. I especially owe these people my gratitude for the arduous task of debugging my manuscript and suggesting changes. Second, for giving me suggestions and generously allowing me to use various items for the cover photo, I would like to express my appreciation to: Hoang-Hang Mai, Chi Thi Pham, Lamoon Suwanna, Veleda Furtado, Lisa Sassi, Paula Hanna, Darlene Burt, Rieko Tsukagoshi, Lynn Tungseth, Judi Hurley, Tan Duc Grocery, and Tilden. Third, for moral and technical support, I would like to thank: my mother, Kang Siu Tjen, my father, Ang Bun Pit, Ang Sen Hoo, Paul Marcius Ang, Ang Sen Long, Rosanne Riley, Carl Bissonnette, Gerald Zampa, Kristen Smith, Chi Thi Pham, Lynn Smith, Christina Taran, David Keene, Richard Middlebrook, Mary Lou Thompson, Libby Bowman, Hanifa Yahiaoui, Carla Ferreira, Rose Rentz, Ramona Delgado, Lourdes Romao, Janusz and Malgorzata Mydlarczyk. Finally, I would like to thank all my cooking class students and friends for encouraging me to undertake this project. To all of the above, I offer my sincere thanks and gratitude.

Eng Tie Ang

Eng Tie Ang

Introduction

I first became aware of Vietnamese cuisine just after I met my husband in 1978. We were both in Idaho at the time and he mentioned how wonderfully delicious the food in Vietnam was when he was there as a soldier in the 60's. Always interested in new and different cuisines, I couldn't wait to try some of this food that he seemed so fond of. As fate would have it, we moved to Seattle in 1980, at a time when many Indochinese refugees were being resettled here. Naturally, in the 16 years we've been here, we have been able to sample this lovely cuisine in many fine restaurants, as well as in the homes of many wonderful Vietnamese friends whom we have made. There has been nothing over the years to make me disagree with my husband's appraisal of Vietnamese cuisine: it is, in fact, wonderfully delicious.

Vietnam is an ancient country with strong traditions and customs. It is one of the world's cradles of civilization, with some of the oldest human fossils having been found in the deep south. Though it has its own unique culture, it has been greatly influenced by its huge neighbor to the north, China. However, it has always been fiercely independent of its sometimes domineering "mother," having had to apologize at least five times over the centuries for defeating China's invading armies! It has also been influenced by India, especially in the south where for centuries traders stopped. France entered Vietnam's history in the 19th Century as a Western colonial power, actually incorporating it into the French Empire in 1884. France's strongest influences on Vietnam were the French language and, more importantly, French bread. So there you have Vietnam's most dominant foreign influences: China, India, and France. I can't really imagine having three better countries to influence an already delightful cuisine. Perhaps the three most important and impressive characteristics of Vietnamese cuisine are the freshness of the ingredients, the creativity of the recipes, and the artful presentation of the food. People are always struck by the abundance of raw fresh vegetables and herbs that are usually a big part of the main cooked dish. It seems that with every meal there is a large assortment of fresh, green aromatic condiments (lettuce, basil, mint, peppers, lime wedges, etc.) sitting on the table waiting to be added to a steaming dish. Vietnamese recipes, in general, are not that difficult to prepare; however, they are cleverly conceived. For example, the various "phos," popular rice-noodle soups, are quite easy and quick to make in their basic form, but by adding fresh ingredients and noodles as one eats, they become an interesting and delightful culinary experience. The multi-sensory presentation of Vietnamese dishes is also a lovely experience for those sitting at the dinner table as the dishes arrive. The wonderful colors and smells, as well as the delicately cut and arranged dishes and condiments harmoniously arranged, immediately greet the diner's eyes and nose.

Generally speaking, Vietnamese recipes often center around meat as the principal element in a meal, with pork being the most popular in the southern regions and beef in the north. The central region is most famous for its hot and spicy recipes. Seafood recipes most often come from the southern regions. Chicken and duck recipes are found throughout the country, as well as tofu, soybean curd, a very common, high-protein, meat substitute.

Therefore, let me conclude by wishing you great enjoyment and pleasure as you try some of these recipes that I have gathered from friends and chefs in the Seattle area. Impress your family and guests with the lovely and delicious presentations that will not only please their palates, but also their eyes and noses. I know that they and you too will come away feeling the same way my husband did so many years ago: happy, satisfied, and impressed.

About the Author

Eng Tie Ang was born in Indonesia of Chinese parents, moved to Brazil at the age of five, and came to the United States at the age of twenty-five. She learned cooking at an early age at home and in her parents' small restaurant in Suzano, Sao Paulo, Brazil. Her first and most influential cooking teacher was her mother, a master of many kinds of Oriental cooking. When Ms. Ang was a teenager, she attended a cooking school in her hometown, specializing in Western cooking. In addition to **Delightful Vietnamese Cooking**, she has also published three other cookbooks: **Delightful Thai Cooking**, **Delightful Brazilian Cooking**, and **Delightful Tofu Cooking**. **Delightful Chinese Cooking**, **Delightful Indonesian Cooking**, and **Delightful Italian Cooking** are forthcoming. Another title to her credit is a children's cultural reader entitled, **The Chinese Lantern Festival**.

In addition to writing cookbooks, Ms. Ang is a cooking instructor for the University of Washington's Experimental College. She also frequently teaches courses through the Puget Consumers' Co-op and other cooking schools in the Seattle area. She has offered courses in Vietnamese cooking, Thai cooking, tofu cooking, vegetarian cooking, Indonesian cooking, Northern Italian cooking and Brazilian cooking. She also does catering for special events and is a food consultant. Moreover, she is an avid organic gardener and an accomplished batik painter.

Ms. Ang lives in Seattle with her husband, Donald Richard Bissonnette, and two sons, Alex and André.

CHAPTER ONE

CONDIMENTS
&
SAUCES

CHAPTER ONE

Condiments and Sauces

DEEP-FRIED SHALLOTS

2 cups canola oil
10 large shallots, thinly
  sliced

Heat the oil in a large wok and deep-fry the shallots for 3 to 5 minutes or until light golden brown and crisp. Drain the shallots on paper towels and let them cool completely. Store them in an airtight container. Used as a garnish on soups and salads.

Makes 2 cups.

MIXED VEGETABLE PICKLES

2 cups green cabbage, cut
  into 1-inch squares
2 large carrots, peeled, cut
  into 2-inch wedges,
  lengthwise
2 cucumbers, peeled, cut
  into 2-inch wedges,
  lengthwise
3 teaspoons salt
1/2 cup sugar
1 cup white wine vinegar

In a small, deep bowl, mix 1 teaspoon of salt with the cabbage by rubbing the salt in and letting the cabbage sit for 5 minutes. Rinse the salt off with cold water and drain the cabbage in a colander. Follow the same procedure with the carrots and cucumbers. In a large bowl, mix the cabbage, carrots, cucumbers, sugar, and vinegar. Refrigerate the pickles before serving. Serve with Vietnamese Barbecued Chicken (see page 34).

Serves 4-6.

13

ROASTED RICE POWDER

1 cup white long grain rice (uncooked)

Place the rice in a dry wok and heat over medium-high heat, stirring the rice constantly to keep it from burning and to allow it to develop a uniform deep golden color (about 4 minutes). Then remove it from the heat and let it cool to room temperature. Grind it into a fine powder in a blender or a spice grinder. Used for salads.

Makes 1/2 cup.

WHITE ICICLE RADISH PICKLES

2 large carrots, peeled, cut very thinly into julienne strips
1 small white icicle radish (daikon), cut very thinly into julienne strips
2 cups water
1/4 cup white vinegar
1 tablespoon sugar
1 teaspoon salt

Combine all the ingredients in a large deep bowl. Stir well and marinate the vegetable pickles at least 30 minutes or overnight in a refrigerator. Before serving, drain the liquid. Place the pickles on a large platter and serve with any kind of barbecued meat.

Serves 4-6.

GINGER FISH SAUCE

1 one-inch piece fresh
   ginger, peeled and
   minced
3 cloves garlic, minced
2 fresh, hot, red cayenne
   peppers, minced
2 tablespoons sugar
1/4 cup fish sauce
1/4 cup fresh lime juice
1/2 cup water

In a small bowl, combine the ginger, garlic, cayenne peppers, sugar, fish sauce, lime juice, and water. Refrigerate before serving. Serve with barbecued meat or fish.

Makes 1 cup.

GREEN ONION WITH OIL

1/2 cup canola oil
1 1/2 cups green onion,
   finely chopped
1 teaspoon salt

Heat the oil in a large deep wok and sauté the green onion and salt for 2 minutes. Let cool. Pour the mixture into a small bowl and serve warm with barbecued meat, fish, soups or noodles.

Makes 1 cup.

Hoisin Sauce

1 tablespoon canola oil
1 large leek (white part only),
  finely chopped
1/2 cup canned hoisin
  sauce
1 cup water
1/2 cup roasted peanuts,
  chopped

Heat the oil in a large deep saucepan, add the leek and sauté it for 2 minutes. Add the hoisin sauce and water and simmer for 5 minutes. Let cool. Store in the refrigerator for up to 4 days. Bring the sauce to room temperature before serving and sprinkle with the peanuts. Serve with barbecued meat or vegetables.

Makes 1 1/2 cups.

Lime Sauce

2 fresh, hot, red cayenne
  peppers, chopped
2 tablespoons sugar
3 fresh large limes,
  squeezed
1/2 cup fish sauce

Combine all the ingredients. Stir well and refrigerate before serving. Serve with barbecued meat or vegetables.

Makes 1 cup.

Peanut Sauce

3 cloves garlic, crushed
2 fresh, hot, red cayenne
  peppers, minced
1/4 cup fresh lime juice
2 tablespoons brown sugar
1/2 teaspoon salt
2 tablespoons light soy
  sauce
1/2 teaspoon shrimp paste
  (optional)
1 1/2 cups smooth or
  crunchy peanut butter
2 cups warm water

In a large bowl, thoroughly mix the garlic, cayenne peppers, lime juice, sugar, salt, soy sauce, shrimp paste, peanut butter, and water into a smooth sauce. Serve at room temperature with barbecued meat or vegetables.

Makes 3 cups.

Plum Sauce

6 dried plums, pitted,
  soaked, drained
2 tablespoons fresh lime
  juice
1/4 cup water
1 tablespoon sugar
2 fresh, hot, red cayenne
  peppers, chopped
2 tablespoons canola oil
3 cloves garlic, crushed
1/4 cup canned hoisin
  sauce

In a blender, blend the plums, lime juice, water, sugar, and cayenne peppers into a smooth sauce. Heat the oil in a saucepan, add the garlic, hoisin sauce, and plum sauce. Stir well and simmer for 2 minutes or until the sauce thickens. Serve with Vietnamese Barbecued Chicken (see page 34).

Makes 1 cup.

SAVORY FISH SAUCE

4 fresh, hot, red cayenne
   peppers, chopped
4 cloves garlic, finely
   chopped
2 tablespoons sugar
1/2 cup fish sauce
1/4 cup fresh lime juice
1 cup water
1 large carrot, peeled,
   shredded (optional)

In a small bowl, combine cayenne peppers, garlic, sugar, fish sauce, lime juice, water, and carrot. Stir well and refrigerate. Serve at room temperature. To be used in salads, Spring Rolls (see page 31) or Beef Lemon Grass Satay (see page 24).

Makes 2 cups.

SOY BEAN PASTE SAUCE

1 tablespoon canola oil
3 cloves garlic, minced
2 fresh, hot, red cayenne
   peppers, minced
1/4 cup soy bean paste
   (Brown Rice Miso)
2 tablespoons sugar
1/4 cup water
1/4 cup fresh coriander
   leaves, chopped
1/4 cup roasted peanuts,
   chopped

Heat te oil in a small pan and sauté the garlic until light golden brown. Add the red cayenne peppers, soy bean paste, sugar, and water. Stir well and simmer over low heat until the sauce thickens. Cool and garnish with the coriander leaves and sprinkle with the peanuts. Serve with barbecued meat or vegetables.

Makes 1 cup.

Soy Lime Sauce

juice of 1 lime
1/2 cup sugar
1/2 cup soy sauce
1/2 cup warm water
2 fresh, hot, red cayenne
   peppers, thinly sliced

In a small bowl, combine all the ingredients. Stir well until the sugar is dissolved. Serve with Barbecued Tofu with Vegetables (see page 23).

Makes 1 1/2 cups.

Sweet and Sour Sauce

1 1/2 cups water
1/4 cup sugar
1/4 cup white vinegar
1 teaspoon salt
1/4 cup ketchup
2 tablespoons cornstarch
   mixed with 4 tablespoons
   cold water

Bring the water to a boil in a large pot. Reduce the heat to low and add the sugar, vinegar, salt, and ketchup. Gradually add the cornstarch mixture, stirring well until it becomes slightly thickened. Serve with Deep-Fried Wontons (see page 25).

Makes 2 cups.

SWEET AND SPICY SAUCE

1 tablespoon canola oil
4 fresh, hot, red cayenne
    peppers, minced
1 1/2 cups water
4 cloves garlic, minced
1 cup fish sauce
1/4 cup white vinegar
1 cup brown sugar
juice of 2 limes
1/4 cup roasted peanuts,
    chopped
1/4 cup fresh coriander
    leaves, chopped

Heat the oil in a large pot and sauté the cayenne peppers for a few seconds. Add the water, garlic, fish sauce, vinegar, brown sugar, and lime juice. Reduce the heat to low and simmer for 5 minutes. Let cool. Sprinkle with the peanuts and garnish with the coriander leaves. Serve with Barbecued Tofu Vegetables (see page 23) or Spring Rolls (see page 31).

Makes 2 cups.

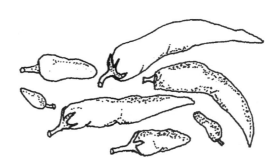

CHAPTER TWO

APPETIZERS

&

SNACKS

CHAPTER TWO

Appetizers and Snacks

Barbecued Tofu with Vegetables

1/4 cup canola oil
1 pkg. extra firm tofu
  (12.4 oz.), drained, cut into
  1-inch thick slices
1 tablespoon sesame oil
1 large leek (white part only),
  finely chopped
1 tablespoon brown sugar
1 teaspoon ground white
  pepper
2/3 cup light soy sauce
juice of 1 lime
1 large onion, cut into 1-inch
  cubes
1 small zucchini, cut into
  1-inch cubes
1 small yellow squash, cut
  into 1-inch cubes
1 large red bell pepper,
  seeded, cut into 1-inch
  cubes
1 lb. fresh mushrooms,
  washed, drained
1 large green bell pepper,
  seeded, cut into 1-inch
  cubes
6" bamboo skewers, soaked
  in water for 15 minutes,
  drained

Heat the oil in a large frying pan and deep-fry the sliced tofu on both sides until golden brown. Let cool and cut into 1-inch cubes. Set aside. In a large, deep bowl, combine the sesame oil, leek, sugar, pepper, soy sauce, and lime juice to make a marinade sauce. Add the fried tofu, onion, zucchini, yellow squash, red bell pepper, mushrooms and green bell pepper and coat all the vegetables well with the mixture and marinate for 20 minutes. Alternate the vegetables and fried tofu cubes on bamboo skewers and broil over a hot charcoal fire for 3 minutes on each side or until cooked thoroughout, or broil in the oven for 3 minutes on each side. Serve with Soy Lime Sauce (see page 19) or Sweet and Spicy Sauce (see page 20).

Serves 4-6.

BEEF LEMON GRASS SATAY

4 cloves garlic, crushed
1 large yellow onion, sliced
2 teaspoons brown sugar
1 teaspoon ground white pepper
1/4 cup fish sauce
2 stems fresh lemon grass, chopped
2 lbs. top sirloin beef, thinly sliced
6" bamboo skewers, soaked in water for 15 minutes, drained
12 green lettuce leaves, washed, drained
1 bunch fresh holy or sweet basil, washed, drained
1 bunch fresh coriander leaves, washed, drained
1 bunch fresh mint leaves, washed, drained
1 large carrot, peeled, shredded

In a blender, blend the garlic, onion, sugar, pepper, fish sauce, and lemon grass into a paste. Pour the paste into a large,deep bowl and add the beef. Marinate the beef for at least 1 hour or overnight in a refrigerator. Put 4 pieces of beef on each skewer and broil over a hot charcoal fire until cooked throughout, or in the broiler for 3 minutes on each side, turning frequently to avoid burning the meat. At the table, each person should take a lettuce leaf, remove the meat from a skewer, and place it on the leaf. On top of the meat, sprinkle a few basil, coriander, and mint leaves. Sprinkle some of the shredded carrot over the top of the leaves. Roll up the leaf tightly and dip it in Savory Fish Sauce (see page 18) and eat it.The same mixture is used for pork, shrimp, and chicken satay.

Serves 4-6.

DEEP-FRIED WONTONS

1 lb. lean ground pork
1 egg, beaten
2 green onions, chopped
3 cloves garlic, minced
1/2 teaspoon salt
1/2 teaspoon ground white
  pepper
1 tablespoon cornstarch
1 tablespoon sesame oil
1 pkg. wonton wrappers
2 cups canola oil for
  deep-frying

In a small bowl, thoroughly mix the pork, egg, green onions, garlic, salt, pepper, cornstarch, and sesame oil. Place 1 teaspoon of the pork mixture in the center of each wonton wrapper. Wet the edges of the wrapper and fold it up, corner to corner, pinching together the 3 corners so that the filled wonton folds up into a triangle. Next, wet one of the bottom corners of the triangle and fold it over to join with the opposite corner with both sides overlapping and then pinching them together (see diagram, page 144). (Another method of filling the wonton wrappers is to wet the four corners and bunch them together to form a flower.) Heat the oil in a wok and deep-fry the wontons for about 2 minutes on each side or until light golden brown. Serve with Savory Fish Sauce (see page 18) or Sweet and Sour Sauce (see page 19).

Serves 4-6.

GROUND SHRIMP ON BREAD

1 lb. shrimp, shelled and deveined (see diagram, page 145)
4 cloves garlic, crushed
2 egg whites
2 tablespoons cornstarch
1/2 teaspoon salt
1/2 teaspoon sugar
1/2 teaspoon ground white pepper
2 green onions, finely chopped
10 slices French bread, crust removed, cut into 2-inch squares
2 cups canola oil for deep- frying

In a blender, blend the shrimp and garlic into a paste. In a bowl, thoroughly mix the shrimp paste with the egg whites, cornstarch, salt, sugar, pepper, and green onions. Spread the shrimp paste about 1/4 inch thick over one side of each slice. Heat the oil in a wok over medium-high heat and carefully drop in 3 bread slices at a time, shrimp side down. (Make sure the oil is hot before dropping in the bread with shrimp.) Deep-fry until golden brown on both sides. Remove and drain on paper towels. Serve with Savory Fish Sauce (see page 18).

Serves 4-6.

SAIGON CHICKEN SANDWICHES

3-4 lb. whole chicken
2 quarts water
1 teaspoon salt
10 cloves garlic, minced
1/2 cup Roasted Rice
   Powder (see page 14),
   or 1 pkg. roasted rice
   powder (3 oz.)
1 teaspoon salt
1/2 teaspoon ground white
   pepper
1 teaspoon sugar
8 French sandwich rolls, cut
   in a half
8 teaspoons mayonnaise
1 large white onion, thinly
   sliced
1 cup fresh coriander leaves
4 fresh red or green cayenne
   peppers, cut in half
1 cucumber, peeled, cut into
   2-inch slices lengthwise
White Icicle Radish Pickles
   (see page 14)
8 teaspoons Maggi
   seasoning sauce

In a large pot, combine the chicken, water and salt and cook for 1 hour or until the chicken is tender. Place the chicken on a large platter and cool. (Reserve the chicken stock for making any desired soup.) Remove and discard the skin and bones from the chicken. Cut the chicken meat into julienne strips and place it into a large bowl. Add the garlic, roasted rice powder, salt, pepper and sugar. Mix well and set aside. Spread one half of a French sandwich roll with 1 teaspoon of mayonnaise. Arrange on top of the roll 2 tablespoons of the chicken mixture, one slice of onion, a few coriander leaves, half of a cayenne pepper, one slice of cucumber, a few Icicle Radish Pickles, and 1 teaspoon of Maggi seasoning sauce. Place the other half of the roll on top. Repeat with each roll.

Serves 8.

Saigon Pork Sandwiches

2 lbs. tenderloin pork
1/2 teaspoon salt
2 tablespoons canola oil
1 pkg. frozen pork skin,
   thawed, soaked in a 2 cups
   of boiling water for 5
   minutes, drained
10 cloves garlic, minced
1/2 cup Roasted Rice
   Powder (see page 14),
   or 1 pkg. roasted rice
   powder (3 oz.)
1/2 teaspoon salt
1/2 teaspoon ground white
   pepper
1 teaspoon sugar
8 French sandwich rolls, cut
   in a half
8 teaspoons mayonnaise
1 large white onion, thinly
   sliced
1 cup fresh coriander leaves
4 fresh red or green cayenne
   peppers, cut in half
1 cucumber, peeled, cut into
   2-inch slices lengthwise
White Icicle Radish Pickles
   (see page 14)
8 teaspoons Maggi
   seasoning sauce

Coat the pork with the salt on both sides. Heat the oil in a large frying pan over low heat and fry the pork on each side for 20 minutes or until the pork is cooked. After the pork has cooled, cut it into julienne strips and place it into a large bowl. Add the pork skin, garlic, roasted rice powder, salt, pepper and sugar. Mix well and set aside. Spread one half of a French sandwich roll with 1 teaspoon of mayonnaise. Arrange on top of the roll 2 tablespoons of the pork mixture, one slice of onion, a few coriander leaves, half of a cayenne pepper, one slice of cucumber, a few Icicle Radish Pickles, and 1 teaspoon of Maggi seasoning sauce. Place the other half of the roll on top. Repeat with each roll.

Serves 8.

SHRIMP BALLS

2 lbs. large shrimp, shelled, deveined (see diagram, page 145)
1/4 lb. lean ground pork
1 teaspoon salt
6 green onions, finely chopped
1 teaspoon minced ginger
2 egg whites
1 tablespoon dry white wine
1/2 teaspoon ground white pepper
1/4 cup cornstarch
2 cups canola oil for deep-frying
2 tablespoons canola oil for oiling the spoon and palm of your hand

In a blender, blend the shrimp into a smooth paste. In a large bowl, thoroughly mix the ground shrimp, ground pork, salt, green onions, ginger, egg whites, wine, white pepper, and cornstarch. Heat the oil in a large wok. Put a little oil on the palm of one hand and place 3 tablespoons of the shrimp mixture in it. Close your hand into a fist and squeeze out an amount about the size of a walnut from the top. Then take an oiled spoon, remove the squeezed out ball and place it on an oiled cookie sheet. Continue squeezing out the shrimp balls in the same way until all the mixture is used. Deep-fry the shrimp balls for 3 to 4 minutes or until golden brown on both sides. Remove and drain on paper towels. Serve with Hoisin Sauce (see page 16), and Mixed Vegetable Pickles (see page 13).

Serves 4-6.

SPICY CHICKEN WITH MINT LEAVES

4 cups water
10 drumsticks
1 small white onion, thinly sliced
1/2 cup fresh mint leaves, finely chopped
1 teaspoon salt
1/2 teaspoon ground white pepper
2 fresh, hot, red cayenne peppers, thinly sliced
4 green onions, finely chopped
1/2 cup fresh coriander leaves, chopped
1/2 cup roasted peanuts, chopped

Bring the water to a boil and add the drumsticks. Simmer for 30 minutes or until the drumsticks are cooked. Discard the water and remove the chicken meat from the bones and shred it. In a small bowl, mix the shredded chicken meat, onion, mint, salt, pepper, cayenne peppers, green onions, and coriander leaves. Sprinkle with the peanuts. Serve with Savory Fish Sauce (see page18), and Mixed Vegetable Pickles (see page 13).

Serves 4-6.

Spring Rolls

4 cloves garlic, minced
1 1/2 lbs. lean ground pork
  or chicken breasts
1 can crab meat (6 1/2 oz.),
  drained
1 small yellow onion, finely
  chopped
2 eggs, beaten
2 large carrots, peeled,
  shredded
1 teaspoon salt
1 teaspoon ground white
  pepper
1 teaspoon sugar
2 tablespoons fish sauce
1 3 1/2 oz. pkg. cellophane
  noodles, soaked in warm
  water for 5 minutes,
  drained, cut into 2-inch
  lengths
1/4 cup dried black fungus
  strips, soaked in warm
  water for 3 minutes,
  drained, chopped
1 pkg. spring roll wrappers
  (25 square wrappers)
1 egg yolk mixed with
  1 tablespoon water (for
  sealing spring rolls)
2 cups canola oil for
  deep-frying

In a large bowl, thoroughly mix the garlic, pork, crab meat, onion, eggs, carrots, salt, pepper, sugar, fish sauce, cellophane noodles, and black fungus strips. Set aside. Separate the spring roll wrappers. Place a wrapper with one corner toward you. On each corner, brush on a little of the egg mixture to seal the edges of the spring roll. Put two tablespoons of the mixture 1/3 of the way from the closest edge. Fold the closest edge over the filling, then fold over the right and left edges, then roll it up very tightly (see diagram, page 146). Continue making the egg rolls until all are ready. Place the finished rolls, seam side down on a large flat serving platter until ready to fry. Do not let them touch each other; otherwise, they will stick together. Heat the oil in a large wok and carefully place 3 rolls at a time in the oil and deep-fry slowly until both sides are golden brown, about 3 minutes each side. (Make sure the oil is hot before deep-frying.) Remove and drain on paper towels. Serve with Savory Fish Sauce (see page 18).

Serves 6-8.

Tofu Corn Fritters

6 fresh ears of corn, shucked
1/2 cup firm tofu, drained,
  crushed
1 small yellow onion,
  chopped
5 cloves garlic, crushed
1 egg, beaten (optional)
1 teaspoon salt
1/2 teaspoon ground white
  pepper
4 green onions, chopped
1/4 cup fresh coriander
  leaves, chopped
1 1/2 cups flour
2 cups canola oil for
  deep-frying

In the blender, blend the corn, tofu, onion, garlic, and egg until finely ground. Pour the mixture into a large bowl and thoroughly mix with the salt, pepper, green onions, coriander leaves, and flour. Heat the oil over medium-high heat in a large wok and drop in a tablespoon of the mixture for each fritter. Deep-fry for 2 minutes or until light golden brown on both sides. Remove and drain on paper towels. Serve hot with Peanut Sauce (see page 17) or Soy Lime Sauce (see page 19).

Serves 6-8.

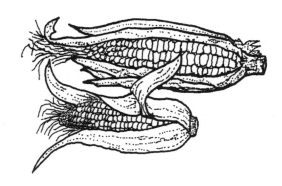

VEGETARIAN SPRING ROLLS

4 cloves garlic, minced
1 small yellow onion, finely chopped
1 pkg. extra firm tofu (12.4 oz.), cut into julienne strips
1 lb. taro root, peeled, shredded
2 small potatoes, peeled, shredded
1 large carrot, peeled, shredded
1 large leek (white part only), chopped
1 teaspoon salt
1 3 1/2 oz. pkg. cellophane noodles, soaked in warm water for 5 minutes, drained, cut into 2-inch lengths
1/4 cup dried black fungus strips soaked in warm water for 3 minutes, drained, chopped
1 pkg. spring roll wrappers (25 square wrappers)
1 egg yolk mixed with 1 tablespoon water (for sealing spring rolls)
2 cups canola oil for deep-frying
1/4 cup light soy sauce
juice of 1 lime
2 fresh, red cayenne peppers, chopped

In a large bowl, thoroughly mix the garlic, onion, tofu, taro root, potatoes, carrot, leek, salt, cellophane noodles, and black fungus strips. Separate the spring roll wrappers. Place a wrapper with one corner toward you. On each corner brush on a little of the egg mixture to seal the edges of the spring roll. Put two tablespoons of the mixture 1/3 of the way from the closest edge. Fold the closest edge over the filling, then fold the right and left edges over it and roll it up very tightly (see diagram, page 146). Continue making the egg rolls until all are ready. Place the finished rolls, seam side down on a large flat serving platter until ready to fry. Do not let them touch each other; otherwise, they will stick together. In a large wok, heat the oil and carefully place 3 rolls at a time in oil and deep-fry slowly until both sides are golden brown, about 3 minutes each side. (Make sure the oil is hot before deep-frying.) Remove and drain on paper towels. Set aside. In a small bowl, mix the soy sauce, lime juice, and cayenne peppers. Serve the spring rolls with this sauce.

Serves 6-8.

VIETNAMESE BARBECUED CHICKEN

8 cloves garlic, crushed
1 teaspoon honey
1/2 cup light soy sauce
2 tablespoons hoisin sauce
1/4 cup fresh coriander,
  finely chopped
4 lbs. drumsticks

In a bowl, thoroughly mix the garlic, honey, soy sauce, hoisin sauce, and fresh coriander. Add the drumsticks and marinate for 30 minutes or overnight in a refrigerator. Barbecue over a moderate charcoal fire for 30 minutes or until the drumsticks are well-cooked on both sides. Serve with Savory Fish Sauce (see page 18).

Serves 6-8.

VIETNAMESE BARBECUED PORK

1 large yellow onion, sliced
6 cloves garlic, crushed
1 tablespoon brown sugar
1/2 cup fish sauce
1/2 cup peanuts, roasted,
  unsalted, crushed
4 lbs. pork chops

In a blender, blend the onion and garlic into a smooth paste. In a large bowl, thoroughly mix the onion mixture, brown sugar, fish sauce, and peanuts. Add the pork chops. Marinate for 30 minutes or overnight in a refrigerator. Barbecue over a moderate charcoal fire for 30 minutes or until the pork chops are well-cooked on both sides. Serve with Savory Fish Sauce (see page 18).

Serves 6-8.

CHAPTER THREE

SOUPS

Soups

ASPARAGUS AND CRAB MEAT SOUP

3 cups chicken or vegetable broth
2 cups water
1 cup canned crab meat
1/2 lb. fresh green asparagus, cleaned, washed, and cut into 1-inch lengths
2 tablespoons cornstarch, dissolved in a 1/4 cup of cold water
1 egg, beaten
1/2 teaspoon ground white pepper
1 teaspoon salt
4 green onions, chopped

Bring the chicken broth and water to a boil in a large deep pot. Add the crab meat and asparagus and bring it back to a boil for 3 minutes. Pour the cornstarch mixture into the soup and stir well. Continuing to stir, add the beaten egg, pepper, and salt. Simmer for 2 minutes and garnish with the green onions.

Serves 4-6.

CHICKEN AND CRAB MEAT SOUP

5 cups chicken broth
1 lb. boneless chicken breast, skinned, thinly sliced
1 cup canned crab meat
1 cup canned baby corn
2 tablespoons corntarch, dissolved in a 1/4 cup of cold water
1/2 teaspoon ground white pepper
1 teaspoon salt
1/4 cup fresh coriander leaves, chopped

Bring the chicken broth to a boil in a large deep pot. Add the sliced chicken, crab meat, and baby corn and bring it back to a boil for about 3 minutes. Pour the cornstarch mixture, white pepper, and salt into the soup and stir well. Simmer for 2 minutes and garnish with the coriander leaves.

Serves 4-6.

CHICKEN RICE SOUP

1 cup white short grain rice, washed, drained

8 cups water

1/2 teaspoon salt

2 lbs. boneless chicken breast, skinned, thinly sliced

2 tablespoons fresh lime juice, mixed with
1 teaspoon salt

1/4 cup canola oil

1 small yellow onion, finely chopped

3 cloves garlic, crushed

1 teaspoon ground white pepper

4 green onions, finely chopped

1/4 cup celery leaves, finely chopped

1/4 cup fresh coriander leaves, chopped

1 small white onion, thinly sliced

In a large uncovered pot, bring the rice, water and salt to a boil. Reduce the heat to low and simmer for about 40 minutes or until the rice is soft. Set aside. Marinate the chicken in the lime juice with salt for 5 minutes. Heat the oil in a frying pan and sauté the onion and garlic until golden brown. Add the white pepper and marinated chicken and simmer for 10 minutes. In small bowls, put 1 cup of the heated rice broth along with some chicken. Garnish with the green onions, celery leaves, coriander leaves, and sliced white onion to taste.

Serves 4-6.

CHICKEN WITH LILY BUD SOUP

8 cups water
1 lb. boneless chicken
   breast, skinned, thinly
   sliced
1/4 cup lily buds, soaked in
   1/2 cup warm water for 20
   minutes (remove hard
   ends from stems and
   tie each bud into a single
   knot)
1/2 cup cellophane noodles,
   soaked, cut into 4-inch
   lengths
1 tablespoon fish sauce
1/2 teaspoon ground white
   pepper
1/2 teaspoon salt
4 green onions, chopped
1/4 cup fresh coriander
   leaves, chopped

Bring the water to a boil in a large deep pot. Add the sliced chicken, lily buds, cellophane noodles, fish sauce, pepper and salt. Bring the water back to a boil, then simmer for 10 minutes or until the chicken meat is cooked. Garnish with the green onions and coriander leaves.

Serves 6-8.

CORN AND CRAB MEAT SOUP

4 cups chicken broth
1 cup canned crab meat
2 cans creamed corn
   (17 oz. each)
1 teaspoon salt
1/2 teaspoon ground white
   pepper
2 tablespoons cornstarch,
   dissolved in a 1/4 cup of
   cold water
4 green onions, chopped
1/4 cup fresh coriander
   leaves, chopped

Bring the chicken broth to a boil in a large deep pot. Add the crab meat and creamed corn and bring it back to a boil for 2 to 3 minutes. Add the salt, pepper and cornstarch mixture and stir well. Simmer for 2 minutes. Garnish with the green onions and coriander leaves.

Serves 4-6.

CORN AND TOFU SOUR SOUP

2 tablespoons canola oil
3 cloves garlic, crushed
1 small yellow onion,
    chopped
4 cups vegetable broth
1 pkg. firm tofu (16 oz.),
    drained, cubed
1 cup frozen whole corn
2 tablespoons cornstarch,
    dissolved in a 1/4 cup of
    cold water
1 tablespoon sugar
juice of 1 lime
1 teaspoon salt
4 green onions, chopped

Heat the oil in a large deep pot and sauté the garlic and onion until light golden brown. Add the vegetable broth, tofu, and frozen corn and bring it back to a boil for 3 minutes. Continuing to stir, add the cornstarch mixture, sugar, lime juice, and salt. Simmer for 5 minutes and garnish with the green onions.

Serves 4-6.

CUCUMBER SOUP

6 cups water
1 lb. boneless chicken
    breast, skinned, sliced
1 teaspoon salt
1/2 teaspoon ground white
    pepper
2 cucumbers, peeled, sliced
1 tablespoon sesame oil
2 green onions, chopped
2 tablespoons fresh
    coriander, chopped

In a large, deep pot, bring the water to a boil and add the sliced chicken, salt, and pepper. Boil for 8 to 10 minutes. Add the sliced cucumber and simmer for about 3 minutes. Sprinkle with the sesame oil. Garnish with the green onions and coriander leaves.

Serves 4-6.

GROUND PORK AND TARO SOUP

1 lb. lean ground pork
3 cloves garlic, crushed
4 green onions, chopped
1/2 teaspoon ground white
   pepper
1/2 teaspoon salt
1 egg, beaten
6 cups water
1 lb. taro root, peeled, cubed
2 tablespoons fish sauce
1/4 cup fresh coriander
   leaves, chopped

In a small bowl, thoroughly mix the pork, garlic, green onions, pepper, salt, and egg. Shape into 1-inch diameter balls. Set aside. In a large pot, bring the water to a boil. Drop in the pork balls and taro root and simmer for 15 minutes or until the taro is soft. Add the fish sauce and simmer for 2 more minutes. Garnish with the coriander leaves.

Serves 4-6.

Lemon Grass Beef Soup

2 tablespoons canola oil
3 cloves garlic, crushed
1 small yellow onion, finely
  chopped
2 lbs. chuck beef, thinly
  sliced
1 stalk fresh lemon grass,
  cut in half
1/2 teaspoon salt
1/2 teaspoon ground white
  pepper
2 tablespoons fish sauce
6 cups water
4 green onions, chopped
1/4 cup fresh coriander
  leaves, chopped

Heat the oil in a large deep pot and sauté the garlic and onion until golden brown. Add the beef, lemon grass, salt, pepper and fish sauce and sauté for 2 minutes. Add the water and bring to a simmer for 1 hour or until the beef is tender. Garnish with the green onions and coriander leaves.

Serves 4-6.

Mixed Vegetable Soup

6 cups vegetable broth
2 small carrots, peeled,
  sliced
1 lb. cauliflower, cut into
  small florets
1 cup fresh mushrooms,
  washed, drained, sliced
1 small leek, washed,
  chopped
1 teaspoon salt
3 green onions, chopped
1/4 cup fresh coriander
  leaves, chopped

Bring the vegetable broth to a boil in a large deep pot. Add the carrots, cauliflower, mushrooms, leek, and salt. Simmer for 20 minutes or until the vegetables are soft. Garnish with the green onions and coriander leaves.

Serves 4-6.

RICE NOODLES WITH BEEF SOUP

1 four-inch piece fresh
   ginger
2 large yellow onions
3 quarts water
4 lbs. round steak, cut into
   2-inch cubes
1/4 cup star aniseed
1 teaspoon salt
1 pkg. flat rice stick noodles
   (16 oz.)
2 lbs. bean sprouts, washed,
   drained
1 large white onion, thinly
   sliced
4 green onions, chopped
1/4 cup fresh coriander
   leaves, chopped
2 fresh, hot, red cayenne
   peppers, chopped
2 fresh limes, cut into
   wedges

Singe the ginger over a burner on high heat for a few seconds until both sides are slightly burned. Peel the skin with a knife. Repeat this procedure with the yellow onions. Set aside. In a large deep pot, bring the water to a boil. Add the ginger, onions, round steak, aniseed, and salt. Reduce the heat and simmer for 2 hours or until the meat is tender. Set aside. In a pot of boiling water, drop in the flat rice stick noodles for about 1 minute, stirring constantly to prevent the noodles from sticking together. Remove and drain in a colander. Rinse with cold water. In small bowls, put 1 cup of the cooked noodles and 1/4 cup of bean sprouts. Add the beef soup and garnish with the sliced onion, green onions, coriander leaves, and cayenne peppers. Sprinkle the squeezed lime wedges over the top.

Serves 6-8.

SHRIMP SOUR SOUP

2 tablespoons canola oil
2 large tomatoes, cut into
  4 wedges
1 small yellow onion, cut
  into 4 wedges
3 cloves garlic, crushed
1 tablespoon sugar
1 teaspoon salt
6 cups chicken broth
1 can chunk pineapple
  (20 oz.), drained
2 lbs. large shrimp, shelled,
  deveined (see diagram,
  page 145)
2 fresh, hot, red cayenne
  peppers, sliced
juice of 1 lime
4 green onions, chopped
1/4 cup fresh coriander
  leaves, chopped

Heat the oil in a large deep pot and sauté the tomatoes, onion, and garlic for 2 minutes. Add the sugar, salt, chicken broth, pineapple, shrimp, cayenne peppers, and lime juice. Bring to a boil and reduce the heat to low and simmer for 5 minutes or until the shrimp is cooked. Do not overcook. Garnish with the green onions and coriander leaves.

Serves 4-6.

Sweet and Sour Soup

2 tablespoons canola oil
2 large tomatoes, cut into
  4 wedges each
1 tablespoon sugar
1 teaspoon salt
6 cups chicken broth
1 can chunk pineapple
  (20 oz.), drained
2 lbs. seabass, cut into
  2-inch squares
1/4 cup fresh lime juice
4 fresh mint leaves, chopped
4 green onions, chopped

Heat the oil in a large deep pot and sauté the tomatoes, sugar, and salt for 2 minutes or until tomatoes are soft. Add the chicken broth, pineapple, fish, and lime juice. Bring it to a boil and reduce the heat to low. Simmer for 3 minutes or until the fish is cooked. Garnish with the mint and green onions.

Serves 4-6.

Tofu with Soy Bean Paste Soup

6 cups water
1/4 lb. lean pork, thinly
  sliced
1 cup string beans, ends
  removed, cut into 1-inch
  lengths
1 cup water chestnuts, thinly
  sliced
1/4 cup soy bean paste
  (Brown Rice Miso)
1/2 teaspoon ground white
  pepper
1 pkg. fried tofu (10.5 oz.),
  cubed
4 green onions, chopped

Bring the water to a boil in a large deep pot and add the pork, string beans, water chestnuts, soy bean paste, and pepper. Cook over low heat for about 10 minutes. Add the tofu and simmer for 5 minutes. Garnish with the green onions.

Serves 4-6.

Vegetable Beef Soup

2 tablespoons canola oil
2 lbs. top sirloin beef, cut
   into 1-inch cubes
1/2 teaspoon ground white
   pepper
1 teaspoon salt
2 tablespoons soy sauce
8 cups water
2 large carrots, peeled,
   sliced
1 large potato, peeled, cubed
1 small yellow onion, cubed
2 fresh, hot, red cayenne
   peppers, chopped
   (optional)
4 green onions, chopped
1/4 cup fresh coriander
   leaves, chopped

Heat the oil in a large deep pot and sauté the beef with the pepper, salt, and soy sauce for 3 minutes. Add the water and bring it to a boil. Reduce the temperature to low and simmer for 30 minutes. Add the carrots, potato, and onion and simmer for 20 minutes or until the vegetables are tender. Garnish with the cayenne peppers, green onions, and coriander leaves.

Serves 4-6.

VEGETABLE TOFU SOUP

3 tablespoons canola oil
1 pkg firm tofu (16 oz.),
   drained, cut into 1-inch
   slices
6 cups water
1/2 lb. pumpkin, peeled, cut
   into 2-inch cubes
1/2 lb. sweet potato, peeled,
   cut into 2-inch cubes
1 cup raw peanuts, shelled
1/2 cup dried mung beans,
   soaked for 20 minutes,
   drained
1 teaspoon salt
1 cup canned coconut milk
1 oz. cellophane noodles, cut
   into 2-inch lengths
1/4 cup fresh coriander
   leaves, chopped

Heat the oil in a large frying pan and fry the sliced tofu on both sides until golden brown. Cool and cut into julienne strips. Bring the water to a boil in a large deep pot and add the pumpkin, sweet potato, peanuts, mung beans, and salt. Reduce the heat to low and simmer for 30 minutes. Add the coconut milk, cellophane noodles and fried tofu. Bring it to a boil for 2 minutes. Garnish with the coriander leaves.

Serves 4-6.

WONTON SOUP

1/2 lb. lean ground pork
1 egg, beaten
2 tablespoons green onion,
    chopped
1 teaspoon salt
1/2 teaspoon ground white
    pepper
1 tablespoon sesame oil
1 tablespoon cornstarch
1 pkg. wonton wrappers
6 cups chicken broth
2 quarts water
4 green onions, chopped
1/4 cup fresh coriander
    leaves, chopped

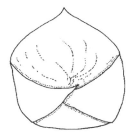

In a small bowl, thoroughly mix the pork, egg, green onion, salt, pepper, sesame oil, and cornstarch. Place 1 teaspoon of the pork mixture in the center of each wonton wrapper. Wet the edges of the wrapper and fold it up, corner to corner, pinching together the 3 corners so that the filled wonton folds up into a triangle. Next, wet one of the bottom corners of the triangle and fold it over to join with the opposite corner with both sides overlapping and then pinching them together (see diagram, page 144). (Another method of filling the wonton wrappers is to wet the four corners and bunch them together to form a flower.) In a large pot, bring the chicken broth to a boil and set it aside. In a deep pot, bring the water to a boil and drop the wontons into the boiling water, uncovered for 3 minutes. When the water boils again, add 1 cup of cold water, then bring it back to a boil for 1 minute. Remove the wontons with a slotted spoon. In small bowls, put 1 cup of the heated chicken broth and add 5 cooked wontons in each bowl. Garnish with the green onions and coriander leaves.

Serves 4-6.

CHAPTER FOUR

SALADS

CHAPTER FOUR

Salads

BEEF SALAD WITH VEGETABLES

1/2 teaspoon salt
1 cucumber, peeled, thinly sliced
1 small white onion, thinly sliced
2 tablespoons canola oil
1 lb. top sirloin beef, thinly sliced
1 fresh lime: peel finely grated; juice squeezed out
2 tablespoons fish sauce
1 tablespoon sugar
1 carrot, peeled, shredded
1 cup celery, thinly sliced
1 fresh, hot, red cayenne pepper, sliced (optional)
1/2 cup roasted peanuts, chopped
1/4 cup fresh coriander, chopped

In a small bowl, combine the salt with the cucumber and onion by rubbing the salt in for 1 minute. Set aside for 5 minutes, then drain out any resulting liquid in a colander. Refrigerate. Heat the oil in a large frying pan and sit-fry the beef for 5 minutes, stirring occasionally. Remove from the heat and let cool. Set aside. In a small bowl, mix the grated lime peel, lime juice, fish sauce, and sugar. Combine the cucumber, onion and beef on a serving platter and pour the sauce over it. Mix well and refrigerate. Just before serving, mix the carrot, celery, cayenne pepper, and peanuts with the beef mixture. Garnish with the coriander leaves.

Serves 4-6.

CARROT SALAD

1 cup water
2 tablespoons rice vinegar
1 tablespoon sugar
1 teaspoon salt
4 large carrots, peeled,
shredded

In a small bowl, combine the water, rice vinegar, sugar, and salt. Stir until the sugar and salt are dissolved. Add the shredded carrots. Cover and refrigerate overnight. Drain the shredded carrots in a colander. Serve at room temperature in individual bowls. It can be eaten as is as a condiment with any meal or it can be added to Savory Fish Sauce (see page 18).

Serves 4.

CARROT AND CUCUMBER SALAD

2 cups water
juice of 2 limes
1 tablespoon sugar
1 teaspoon salt
2 large carrots, peeled,
shredded
2 small cucumbers, peeled,
shredded

In a small bowl, combine the water, lime juice, sugar, and salt. Stir until the sugar and salt are dissolved. Add the shredded carrots and cucumbers. Cover and refrigerate overnight. Drain the shredded carrots and cucumber in a colander. Serve at room temperature in individual bowls. It can be eaten as is as a condiment with any meal, or it can be added to Savory Fish Sauce (see page 18).

Serves 4.

CARROT WITH TOFU SALAD

1/4 cup canola oil
1 pkg. extra firm tofu
(12.4 oz.), drained, cut
into 1-inch slices
2 large carrots, peeled, cut
into thin julienne strips
2 stalks celery, peeled, cut
into thin julienne strips
1 cucumber, peeled, cut into
julienne strips
1 tablespoon sugar
1 teaspoon salt
2 fresh, hot, red cayenne
peppers, thinly sliced
3 tablespoons rice vinegar
1/2 teaspoon ground white
pepper
juice of 1 lime
1/4 cup fresh coriander
leaves, chopped
1/2 cup roasted unsalted
peanuts, chopped

Heat the oil in a large frying pan and fry the sliced tofu on both sides until golden brown. Cool and cut into 1-inch squares. In a large salad bowl, mix the fried tofu, carrots, celery, cucumber, sugar, salt, cayenne peppers, rice vinegar, white pepper and lime juice. Refrigerate for 10 minutes before serving. Garnish with the coriander leaves and sprinkle with the peanuts.

Serves 4-6.

Jicama with Tofu Salad

1/4 cup canola oil
1 pkg. extra firm tofu
 (12.4 oz.), drained, cut
 into 1-inch slices
2 large carrots, peeled, cut
 into thin julienne strips
1 lb. jicama, peeled, cut into
 thin julienne strips
1/4 cup fresh coriander
 leaves, chopped
4 fresh mint leaves, chopped
2 fresh, hot, red cayenne
 peppers, thinly sliced
1 tablespoon sugar
1 teaspoon salt
3 tablespoons rice vinegar
juice of 1 lime
1/2 cup roasted, unsalted
 peanuts, chopped

Heat the oil in a large frying pan and fry the sliced tofu on both sides until golden brown. Cool and cut into 1-inch squares. In a large salad bowl, mix the fried tofu, carrots, jicama, coriander leaves, mint leaves, cayenne peppers, sugar, salt, rice vinegar, and lime juice. Sprinkle with the peanuts.

Serves 4-6.

KOHLRABI SALAD

juice of 1 lime
2 tablespoons sugar
1/4 cup fish sauce
3 tablespoons rice vinegar
2 fresh, hot, red cayenne
  peppers, thinly sliced
2 cups water
1 lb. large shrimp, shelled,
  deveined (see diagram,
  page145)
3 kohlrabies, peeled,
  shredded
1 large carrot, peeled,
  shredded
1/4 cup fresh mint leaves
1/2 cup fresh coriander
  leaves, chopped
1/2 cup roasted, unsalted,
  peanuts, chopped

In a small bowl, combine the lime juice, sugar, fish sauce, rice vinegar, and cayenne peppers. Stir until the sugar is dissolved. Set aside. Bring the water to a boil in a small pot. Cook the shrimp in the boiling water for 2 minutes or until tender. Do not overcook. Drain and cool. Cut the shrimp in half lengthwise and set them aside. Place the kohlrabies and carrot on a large serving platter. Arrange the sliced shrimp on top. Pour the dressing over the salad and garnish with the mint leaves and coriander leaves. Sprinkle with the peanuts.

Serves 4-6.

PORK AND SHRIMP VEGETABLE SALAD

4 cups water
1/2 lb. pork shoulder
1 lb. large shrimp, shelled, deveined (see diagram, page 145)
1/4 cup fish sauce
1/4 cup fresh lime juice
2 tablespoons sugar
3 cloves garlic, minced
1 fresh, hot, red cayenne pepper, chopped (optional)
2 large carrots, peeled, shredded
2 cucumbers, peeled, cut into julienne strips
1/4 cup fresh coriander leaves, chopped
1/4 cup fresh mint leaves
1/4 cup roasted, unsalted, peanuts, chopped

Bring 2 cups of water to a boil in a small pot and cook the pork in the boiling water for 20 minutes or until tender. Drain and cool. Slice the pork thinly. Set aside. Bring the remaining water to a boil in another small pot and cook the prawns in the boiling water for 2 minutes or until tender. Do not overcook. Drain and cool. Cut the shrimp in half lengthwise and set them aside. In a small bowl, combine the fish sauce, lime juice, sugar, garlic, and cayenne pepper. Stir well until the sugar is dissolved. Set aside. Place the shredded carrots and cucumbers on a large serving platter. Arrange the sliced pork and shrimp in layers on top. Pour the dressing over the salad and garnish with the coriander leaves and mint leaves. Sprinkle with the peanuts.

Serves 4-6.

SHRIMP SALAD

2 cups water
2 lbs. large shrimp, shelled,
  deveined (see diagram,
  page 145)
1 cucumber, peeled, cut into
  julienne strips
2 large carrots, peeled,
  shredded
2 tablespoons sugar
1/4 cup fish sauce
1/4 cup fresh lime juice
3 tablespoons rice vinegar
2 fresh, hot, red cayenne
  peppers, chopped
1 tablespoon roasted
  sesame seeds
1/4 cup fresh mint leaves
1/4 cup fresh coriander
  leaves, chopped

Bring the water to a boil in a deep pot and cook the shrimp in the boiling water for 2 minutes or until tender. Do not overcook. Drain and cool. Cut the shrimp in half lengthwise and set them aside. On a serving platter, arrange the cooked shrimp, cucumber, and carrots in layers. Set aside. In a small bowl, thoroughly mix the sugar, fish sauce, lime juice, rice vinegar, and cayenne peppers. Just before serving, pour the dressing over the salad. Sprinkle with the roasted sesame seeds and garnish with the mint leaves and coriander leaves.

Serves 4-6.

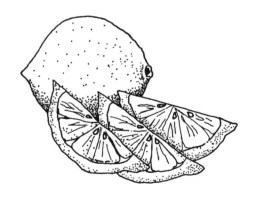

Spicy Chicken Salad

4 cups water
2 lbs. boneless chicken
    breasts, skinned
2 cucumbers, peeled,
    shredded
3 cloves garlic, minced
1/4-inch sliced fresh ginger,
    cut into julienne strips
4 green onions, chopped
2 fresh, hot, red cayenne
    peppers, minced (optional)
2 tablespoons sesame oil
2 tablespoons soy sauce
1/2 teaspoon salt
1 teaspoon sugar
1/2 teaspoon ground white
    pepper
2 tablespoons fresh lime
    juice
1/4 cup fresh coriander
    leaves, chopped
2 green onions, finely
    chopped

Bring the water to a boil in a large deep pot and put the chicken breasts into the boiling water and cook for 30 minutes or until the chicken is done. Remove the chicken and place it on a plate. After it has cooled, shred the chicken into small pieces. Place the shredded chicken and shredded cucumber on a large serving platter. In a small bowl, thoroughly mix the garlic, ginger, green onions, cayenne peppers, sesame oil, soy sauce, salt, sugar, pepper, and lime juice. Pour the mixture over the chicken and cucumbers. Garnish with the coriander leaves and green onions.

Serves 4-6.

Vietnamese Chicken Salad

4 cups water
2 lbs. boneless chicken
  breasts, skinned
1/4 cup fresh lime juice
1 tablespoon sugar
1 teaspoon salt
2 dried, hot, red cayenne
  peppers, finely chopped
2 cups green cabbage,
  shredded
1/4 cup roasted peanuts,
  chopped
1/4 cup fresh coriander
  leaves, chopped

Bring the water to a boil in a deep pot and put the chicken breasts into the boiling water and cook for 30 minutes or until done. Remove and cool. Shred the chicken breasts into small pieces. Set aside. In a small bowl, mix the lime juice, sugar, salt, and cayenne peppers. Set aside. Place the shredded chicken and cabbage on a large serving platter. Pour the lime juice mixture over the chicken and cabbage. Sprinkle with the peanuts and garnish with the coriander leaves.

Serves 4-6.

WHITE ICICLE RADISH SALAD

juice of 1 lime
2 tablespoons sugar
1/4 cup fish sauce
3 tablespoons rice vinegar
2 fresh, hot, red cayenne
   peppers, thinly sliced
2 cups water
1 lb. large shrimp, shelled,
   deveined (see diagram,
   page 145)
1 large white icicle radish
   (daikon), peeled, cut into
   julienne strips
1 large carrot, peeled, cut
   into julienne strips
1 large white onion,
   thinly sliced
1/4 cup fresh mint leaves
1/2 cup fresh coriander
   leaves, chopped
1/2 cup roasted, unsalted
   peanuts, chopped

In a small bowl, combine the lime juice, sugar, fish sauce, rice vinegar, and cayenne peppers. Stir until the sugar is dissolved. Set aside. Bring the water to a boil in a small pot and cook the shrimp in the boiling water for 2 minutes or until tender. Do not overcook. Drain and cool. Cut the shrimp in half lengthwise and set them aside. On a serving platter, arrange the cooked shrimp, radish, carrot, and onion in layers. Just before serving, pour the dressing over the salad and garnish with the mint leaves and coriander leaves. Sprinkle with the peanuts.

Serves 4-6.

CHAPTER FIVE

VEGETABLES

Vegetables

BLACK MUSHROOMS WITH TOFU

1/2 cup canola oil for
   deep- frying
1 pkg. firm tofu (16 oz.),
   drained, cubed
3 tablespoons sesame oil
3 cloves garlic, crushed
8 dried black Chinese
   mushrooms, soaked in
   1/4 cup of warm water
   for 10 minutes, cut into
   julienne strips (Note:
   Discard the hard ends
   from the stems and the
   soaking water.)
1 teaspoon salt
1/2 teaspoon ground
   black pepper
10 green onions, cut into
   2-inch lengths
1 cup unsalted, roasted
   cashew nuts
1/4 cup fresh coriander
   leaves, chopped

Heat the oil in a wok and deep-fry the tofu until golden brown on both sides. Remove and drain on paper towels. Set aside. Heat the sesame oil in a large frying pan and sauté the garlic, black Chinese mushrooms and salt for 2 minutes. Add the pepper, fried tofu, green onions, and cashew nuts and stir-fry for 1 minute. Garnish with the coriander leaves.

Serves 4-6.

CAULIFLOWER WITH BABY CORN

2 tablespoons canola oil
3 cloves garlic, crushed
1 small onion, finely
  chopped
2 cups cauliflower florets
1 can baby corn (15 oz.),
  drained
2 tablespoons light soy
  sauce
1/4 cup fresh coriander
  leaves, chopped

Heat the oil in a large wok over high heat and sauté the garlic and onion until light golden brown. Add the cauliflower, baby corn, and soy sauce. Reduce the heat to low and simmer, covered, for 2 to 3 minutes or until the cauliflower is cooked. Garnish with the coriander leaves.

Serves 4-6.

CAULIFLOWER WITH MUSHROOMS

2 tablespoons canola oil
3 cloves garlic, crushed
2 cups cauliflower florets
1 large carrot, peeled,
  thinly sliced
3 tablespoons fish sauce
1 cup fresh mushrooms,
  washed, drained, sliced
1/4 cup fresh coriander
  leaves, chopped

Heat the oil in a large wok over a high heat and sauté the garlic until light golden brown. Add the cauliflower, carrot, and fish sauce. Reduce the heat to low and simmer, covered, for 2 to 3 minutes. Add the mushrooms and simmer for 2 minutes. Garnish with the coriander leaves.

Serves 4-6.

CURRIED MOCK CHICKEN

3 cloves garlic, crushed
2 tablespoons brown sugar
2 tablespoons soy sauce
  or fish sauce
1 large yellow onion, sliced
1 stalk fresh lemon grass,
  finely chopped
2 tablespoons canola oil
2 cups fresh or frozen
  gluten, thawed
  (You can use canned
  braised gluten instead of
  fresh or frozen. If you use
  canned gluten, make sure
  to omit the brown sugar;
  otherwise, it will be too
  sweet.)
1 large carrot, peeled, sliced
1/2 teaspoon ground black
  pepper
2 fresh, hot, red cayenne
  peppers, sliced
2 tablespoons curry powder
1 can coconut milk
  (14 fl. oz.)
1/4 cup fresh coriander
  leaves, chopped

In a blender, blend the garlic, sugar, soy sauce, onion, and lemon grass into a smooth paste. Set aside. Heat the oil in a medium-sized pot and stir-fry the fresh gluten, carrot, black pepper, cayenne peppers, and curry powder for 2 minutes, stirring occasionally. Add the lemon grass mixture and coconut milk and simmer for 10 minutes. Garnish with the coriander leaves. Serve warm over rice.

Serves 4-6.

Green Beans with Tofu

3 tablespoons canola oil
1 pkg. extra firm tofu (12.4 oz.), cut into 1-inch cubes
1 small yellow onion, thinly sliced
2 large tomatoes, cut into 4 wedges
1 tablespoon sugar
2 tablespoons soy sauce
1 cup canned sliced bamboo shoots
1 lb. string beans, ends removed, sliced
2 fresh, hot, red cayenne peppers, sliced
1/4 cup fresh coriander leaves, chopped

Heat 2 tablespoons of oil in a large frying pan and fry the cubed tofu until golden brown on both sides. Remove and drain on paper towels. Set aside. In a large wok, heat 1 tablespoon of oil over medium-high heat and stir-fry the onion for 2 minutes or until light golden brown. Add the tomatoes, sugar, soy sauce, bamboo shoots, string beans, cayenne peppers, and fried tofu. Reduce the heat to low, cover, and simmer for 5 minutes or until the string beans are tender. Garnish with the coriander leaves. Serve warm over rice.

Serves 4-6.

LEMON GRASS MOCK CHICKEN

3 cloves garlic, crushed
2 tablespoons brown sugar
2 tablespoons soy sauce or
   fish sauce
1 stalk fresh lemon grass,
   finely chopped
2 tablespoons canola oil
1 large white onion, sliced
2 cups fresh or frozen
   gluten, thawed
   (You can use canned
   braised gluten instead of
   fresh or frozen. If you use
   canned gluten, make sure
   to omit the brown sugar;
   otherwise, it will be too
   sweet.)
1/2 teaspoon ground white
   pepper   (
2 fresh, hot, red cayenne
   peppers, sliced
4 green onions, cut into
   2-inch lengths
1/4 cup roasted peanuts,
   chopped

In a blender, blend the garlic, sugar, soy sauce, and lemon grass into a smooth paste. Set aside. Heat the oil in a large wok and stir-fry the onion, gluten, white pepper, and cayenne peppers for 3 minutes, stirring occasionally. Add the lemon grass mixture and green onions and stir-fry for 2 minutes, stirring frequently. Sprinkle with the peanuts. Serve warm over rice.

Serves 4-6.

Mixed Vegetables with Lemon Grass

3 tablespoons canola oil

1 pkg. extra firm tofu (12.4 oz.), cut into 1-inch cubes

1 stalk fresh lemon grass, cut into 2-inch lengths

1 large leek (white part only), finely chopped

1 green bell pepper, seeded, cut into 1-inch cubes

1 red bell pepper, seeded, cut into 1-inch cubes

1/4 lb. green cabbage, cut into 1-inch cubes

1 cup fresh mushrooms, washed, drained

1 large carrot, peeled, thinly sliced

1 can baby corn (15 oz.), drained

1/2 teaspoon salt

2 tablespoons soy sauce

1 tablespoon sugar

1/4 cup fresh coriander leaves, chopped

Heat 2 tablespoons of oil in a large frying pan and fry the cubed tofu until golden brown on both sides. Remove and drain on paper towels. Set aside. In a large pot, heat 1 tablespoon of oil over medium-high heat and sauté the lemon grass and leek for 2 minutes. Add the green bell pepper, red bell pepper, cabbage, mushrooms, carrot, baby corn, salt, soy sauce, sugar, and fried tofu. Cover and simmer for 5 minutes or until the vegetables are cooked. Garnish with the coriander leaves.

Serves 4-6.

MIXED VEGETABLES WITH TOFU

3 tablespoons canola oil
1 pkg. extra firm tofu
   (12.4 oz.), drained, cut into
   1-inch cubes
1 leek, thinly sliced
2 cups cauliflower florets
1 cup string beans,
   ends removed,
   cut into 2-inch lengths
1 can coconut milk
   (14 fl. oz.)
1 teaspoon salt
1/2 teaspoon ground white
   pepper
1 fresh, hot, red cayenne
   pepper, sliced (optional)
4 tablespoons fresh
   coriander leaves, chopped

Heat 2 tablespoons of oil in a large frying pan and fry the cubed tofu until golden brown on both sides. Remove and drain on paper towels. Set aside. In a large pot, heat 1 tablespoon of oil over medium-high heat. Stir-fry the leek, cauliflower, and string beans for 3 minutes, stirring occasionally. Add the coconut milk, salt, pepper, cayenne pepper, and fried tofu. Cover the pot and simmer for 5 minutes or until the vegetables are cooked. Garnish with the coriander leaves.

Serves 4-6.

SPICY FRIED TOFU

1/4 cup canola oil for
   deep-frying
1 pkg. firm tofu (16 oz.),
   drained, cubed
2 tablespoons canola oil
1 stalk fresh lemon grass,
   minced
1 large white onion, sliced
3 cloves garlic, crushed
3 fresh, hot, red cayenne
   peppers, sliced
1/4 lb. tenderloin pork, thinly
   sliced
3 tablespoons fish sauce
1 tablespoon brown sugar
1/2 teaspoon ground white
   pepper
4 green onions, cut into
   2-inch lengths
1/4 cup fresh coriander
   leaves, chopped
1/4 cup roasted peanuts,
   chopped

Heat the oil in a large frying pan and deep-fry the tofu until golden brown on both sides. Remove and drain on paper towels. Set aside. Heat the oil in a wok and stir-fry the lemon grass, onion, garlic, cayenne peppers, and pork for 3 minutes or until the pork is cooked, stirring occasionally. Add the fish sauce, sugar, pepper, green onions, and fried tofu and stir-fry for 1 minute. Garnish with the coriander leaves and sprinkle with the peanuts.

Serves 4-6.

STEAMED CHINESE BLACK MUSHROOMS

6 dried black Chinese
mushrooms, soaked in
1/4 cup of warm water
for 10 minutes
(reserve the water),
cut into julienne strips
(Note: Remove the hard
ends from the stems.)

1 tablespoon finely
shredded fresh ginger

1/4 cup dried shrimp, soaked
in 1/2 cup of warm water
for 5 minutes (reserve
the water)

1 pkg. firm tofu (16 oz.),
drained, cubed

3 cloves garlic, crushed

1/4 lb. boneless chicken
breast, skinned, thinly
sliced

3 tablespoons fish sauce

1/2 teaspoon ground white
pepper

2 green onions, finely
chopped

1/4 cup fresh coriander
leaves, chopped

In a large deep bowl, mix the black Chinese mushrooms, reserved mushroom soaking water, ginger, dried shrimp, reserved shrimp soaking water, tofu, garlic, chicken, fish sauce, and pepper. Pour the mixture in a large heat-proof bowl and place in a steamer and cook for 15-20 minutes or until chicken is tender. Garnish with the green onions and coriander leaves.

Serves 4-6.

Steamed Tofu with Green Onion

1 pkg. firm tofu (16 oz.),
  drained, cut into 1-inch
  cubes
3 tablespoons soy sauce
4 green onions, chopped
1 tablespoon sesame oil
1/4 teaspoon ground white
  pepper
1/4 teaspoon crushed red
  pepper flakes
1/4 cup fresh coriander
  leaves, chopped

In a small heat-resistant bowl, mix the tofu, soy sauce, green onions, sesame oil, pepper, and pepper flakes. Place the bowl into a bamboo steamer and cover. Steam over medium heat for 10 minutes. Garnish with the coriander leaves. Serve warm over rice.

Serves 4.

Stir-Fried Bean Sprouts with Shrimp

1/2 lb. fresh large shrimp,
  shelled, deveined
  (see diagram, page 145)
1 tablespoon fish sauce
1/2 teaspoon ground
  black pepper
2 tablespoons canola oil
3 cloves garlic, crushed
3 cups fresh bean sprouts
1/2 teaspoon salt
4 green onions, chopped
1/4 cup fresh coriander
  leaves, chopped

In a small bowl, marinate the shrimp with fish sauce and pepper for 10 minutes. Heat the oil in a wok and stir-fry the shrimp with garlic for 2 minutes, then add the bean sprouts, salt, and green onions and stir-fry for 1 minute. Garnish with the coriander leaves.

Serves 4-6.

STUFFED CABBAGE WITH TOFU

3 quarts water
1 large green cabbage, washed
2 lbs. lean ground pork
1 egg, beaten
4 green onions, chopped
1/2 teaspoon ground black pepper
3 cloves garlic, minced
1 teaspoon salt
1 teaspoon sugar
1 tablespoon fish sauce (optional)
1 tablespoon cornstarch
1 tablespoon sesame oil
1 pkg. firm tofu (16 oz.), drained, mashed

Bring the water to a boil in a deep pot and plunge the cabbage into the boiling water for 2 to 3 minutes. Use a slotted spoon to remove the cabbage from the water. Carefully remove the outer leaves. Repeat this process 2 to 3 times or until all the leaves have been removed. Discard the water. In a large deep bowl, thoroughly mix the pork, egg, green onions, pepper, garlic, salt, sugar, fish sauce, cornstarch, sesame oil, and tofu. Spread the stuffing over each leaf, leaving a 1-inch border uncovered around the edges. Roll the leaves, enclosing the stuffing. Place the stuffed cabbage leaves in a large bamboo steamer and steam for 15 minutes. Serve with Savory Fish Sauce (see page 18).

Serves 6-8.

STUFFED GREEN PEPPERS WITH SHRIMP

2 lbs. fresh large shrimp, shelled, deveined (see diagram, page 145)
1 small yellow onion, finely chopped
1 teaspoon salt
3 cloves garlic, crushed
1 tablespoon cornstarch
1/2 teaspoon ground white pepper
1 teaspoon fresh ginger, minced
4 medium green bell peppers, seeded, cut lengthwise

In a blender, blend the shrimp into a paste. Pour the paste in a small bowl and add the onion, salt, garlic, cornstarch, pepper, and ginger. Mix well and stuff the mixture into the peppers. Cook in a bamboo steamer over high heat for 30 minutes or until the stuffed peppers are cooked. Serve with Savory Fish Sauce (see page 18).

Serves 4-6.

STUFFED TOMATOES WITH PORK

4 medium-sized, firm red tomatoes
1/2 lb. ground pork
3 cloves garlic, crushed
2 tablespoons fish sauce
1 egg, beaten
1 tablespoon cornstarch
2 tablespoons canola oil

Cut off the tops and core the tomatoes. Rinse them out with water and set aside. In a small bowl, thoroughly mix the pork, garlic, fish sauce, egg, and cornstarch. Stuff the mixture into the tomatoes. Heat the oil in a large frying pan over a high heat. Place the tomatoes, stuffed sides down, onto the oil. Lower the heat to medium, cover the frying pan, and cook for 3-4 minutes on each side.

Serves 4.

TOFU CURRY

1/2 cup canola oil

2 pkgs. extra firm tofu (12.4 oz. each), drained, cut into 1-inch slices

2 large red bell peppers, seeded, cut into 1-inch cubes

1 small yellow onion, cut into 1-inch cubes

2 tablespoons curry powder

1 fresh, hot, red cayenne pepper, sliced

1 teaspoon salt

1/2 teaspoon ground black pepper

1 cup water

1 can coconut milk (14 fl. oz.)

1/4 cup fresh coriander leaves, chopped

1/4 cup roasted peanuts, chopped

Heat the oil in a large frying pan and fry the sliced tofu until golden brown on both sides. Remove and drain on paper towels. Cool and cut into 1-inch cubes. In a deep pot, add the fried tofu, red bell pepper, onion, curry powder, cayenne pepper, salt, pepper, and water. Cook the vegetables over medium heat for 5 minutes. Add the coconut milk and simmer for 3 minutes. Garnish with the coriander leaves. Sprinkle with the peanuts.

Serves 4-6.

TOFU WITH BLACK BEAN SAUCE

2 tablespoons canola oil
3 cloves garlic, crushed
1 teaspoon finely grated
   ginger
2 tablespoons salted black
   beans (Chinese style)
1 small stalk leek, thinly
   sliced
1 fresh, hot, red cayenne
   pepper, sliced
1 pkg. firm tofu (16 oz.),
   drained, cubed
1 tablespoon soy sauce
1 tablespoon cornstarch,
   dissolved in a 1/4 cup of
   cold water
1 tablespoon sesame oil
4 green onions, chopped
1/4 cup fresh coriander
   leaves, chopped

Heat the oil in a wok and sauté the garlic, ginger and salted black beans for 1 minute. Add the leek, cayenne pepper, tofu, soy sauce, and cornstarch mixture. Stir and simmer for 3 minutes. Sprinkle with the sesame oil. Garnish with the green onions and coriander leaves.

Serves 4-6.

Tofu with Eggplant

3 tablespoons canola oil
1 pkg. extra firm tofu
(12.4 oz.), drained, cut into
1-inch slices
1 large leek (white part only),
finely chopped
1 lb. fresh mushrooms,
washed, drained
2 large fresh tomatoes, cut
into 4 wedges
1 tablespoon tomato paste
2 red bell peppers, seeded,
cut into 1-inch cubes
1 small yellow onion, cut
into 1-inch cubes
1 zucchini, cut into 1-inch
cubes
1 yellow squash, cut into
1-inch cubes
1 large eggplant, cut into
2-inch cubes
1/2 teaspoon salt
1 teaspoon sugar
2 tablespoons soy sauce
1 fresh, hot, red cayenne
pepper, sliced
1/4 cup fresh coriander
leaves, chopped

Heat 2 tablespoons of oil in a large frying pan and fry the sliced tofu until golden brown on both sides. Remove and drain on paper towels. Cool and cut into 1-inch cubes. Set aside. In a large pot, heat 1 tablespoon of oil over medium-high heat. Stir-fry the leek for 2 minutes. Add the mushrooms, tomatoes, tomato paste, peppers, onion, zucchini, yellow squash, eggplant, salt, sugar, soy sauce, cayenne pepper, and fried tofu. Simmer for 10 minutes or until the vegetables are soft. Garnish with the coriander leaves.

Serves 4-6.

TOMATOES STUFFED WITH CRAB

6 firm medium-sized tomatoes
2 cans crab meat (6 1/2 oz. each), drained
1 tablespoon fish sauce
1 teaspoon fresh ginger, minced
1 tablespoon fresh coriander leaves, minced
2 green onions, chopped
1 egg, beaten
1 tablespoon cornstarch
1 teaspoon ground white pepper
1 teaspoon sugar
1 tablespoon sesame oil
1/4 cup fresh coriander leaves, chopped

Cut off the tops of the tomatoes, core them, rinse them out with water, and set them aside. In a small bowl, thoroughly mix the crab meat, fish sauce, ginger, coriander, green onions, egg, cornstarch, white pepper, sugar, and sesame oil. Stuff the mixture into the tomatoes. Place the stuffed tomatoes into an oiled 9x13 inch baking pan and bake in a 350 degree oven for 25 minutes or until the tops are light golden brown. Garnish with the coriander leaves. Serve with Soy Bean Paste (see page 18).

Serves 4-6.

TOMATOES STUFFED WITH TOFU

6 firm medium-sized, red
   tomatoes
1/2 cup firm tofu, drained,
   mashed
1 cup fresh mushrooms,
   washed, drained,
   chopped
3 cloves garlic, minced
4 green onions, chopped
2 tablespoons fish sauce
1/2 teaspoon ground white
   pepper
1 tablespoon cornstarch
1 egg, beaten (optional)
1/4 cup canola oil
1/4 cup fresh coriander
   leaves, chopped

Cut off the tops, core the tomatoes, rinse them out with water and set them aside. In a small bowl, thoroughly mix the tofu, mushrooms, garlic, green onions, fish sauce, pepper, cornstarch, and egg. Stuff the mixture into the tomatoes. Heat the oil in a large frying pan over high heat. Place the tomatoes, stuffed sides down, onto the oil. Lower the heat to medium, cover the frying pan, and cook for 2 to 3 minutes on each side. Garnish with the coriander leaves. Serve with Sweet and Sour Sauce (see page 19).

Serves 4-6.

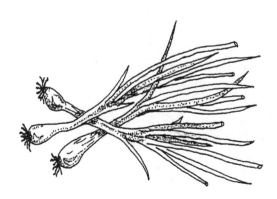

VEGETABLE TOFU CURRY

1/4 cup canola oil for
deep-frying
1 pkg. firm tofu (16 oz.),
drained, cubed
2 stalks fresh lemon grass,
chopped
1 large white onion, sliced
1 tablespoon brown sugar
3 tablespoons fish sauce
1/2 teaspoon salt
1/2 teaspoon ground white
pepper
2 tablespoons canola oil
4 cloves garlic, crushed
2 large tomatoes, chopped
1 lb. eggplant, cubed
1 large red bell pepper,
seeded, cubed
1 large carrot, peeled, sliced
1 lb. string beans, ends
removed, cut into 2-inch
lengths
2 fresh, hot, red cayenne
peppers, sliced
3 tablespoons curry powder
1 can coconut milk
(14 fl. oz.)
1/2 cup fresh coriander
leaves, chopped

Heat the oil in a large frying pan and deep-fry the tofu until golden brown on both sides. Remove and drain on paper towels. Set aside. In a blender, blend the lemon grass, onion, sugar, fish sauce, salt, and pepper into a smooth paste. Set aside. Heat the oil in a large pot and stir-fry the garlic, tomatoes, eggplant, red bell pepper, carrot, string beans, cayenne peppers, and curry powder for 2 minutes. Add the coconut milk, fried tofu, and lemon grass mixture. Simmer for 10 minutes or until the vegetables are done. Do not overcook. Garnish with the coriander leaves. Serve warm over rice.

Serves 4-6.

CHAPTER SIX

SEAFOOD

Seafood

CLAMS WITH BASIL

2 tablespoons canola oil
6 cloves garlic, crushed
2 fresh, hot, red cayenne
  peppers, sliced (optional)
1/2 cup fresh holy or sweet
  basil leaves, washed
2 lbs. fresh clams, washed,
  drained
1/2 cup fish sauce
juice of 1 lime

Heat the oil in a wok and sauté the garlic, cayenne peppers, and basil leaves for 1 minute. Add the clams and fish sauce and stir-fry for 5 minutes over high heat, stirring frequently. Pour onto a large serving platter and sprinkle with the lime juice.

Serves 4-6.

SAVORY CLAMS

2 lbs. fresh clams, washed,
  drained
2 tablespoons canola oil
1 small leek, finely chopped
3 cloves garlic, crushed
1 teaspoon salt
1/2 teaspoon sugar
1 tablespoon brandy
1/2 teaspoon ground black
  pepper
1 fresh, hot, red cayenne
  pepper, finely chopped

Place the clams in a steamer and steam for 3 minutes or until the clam shells open. (Discard clams that do not open.) Remove the clams from shells, retaining the larger shells. In a wok, heat the oil and stir-fry the leek, garlic, salt and sugar for 2 minutes. Add the brandy, pepper, cayenne pepper and clams. Stir-fry for 1 minute. Stuff clam and sauce mixture in each empty, large half shell. Place into 9x13 inch baking pan and broil for 3 minutes or until the tops are light brown.

Serves 4-6.

CRAB OMELETTE

2 tablespoons fish sauce
1/2 teaspoon ground white
  pepper
1 fresh, hot, red cayenne
  pepper, chopped (optional)
1/2 cup canned crab meat
2 tablespoons chopped
  yellow onion
4 green onions, finely
  chopped
2 tablespoons canola oil
5 eggs, beaten
1/4 cup fresh coriander
  leaves, chopped
1/4 cup roasted peanuts,
  chopped

In a small bowl, combine the fish sauce, white pepper, cayenne pepper, crab meat, onion, and green onions. Set aside. Heat the oil in a large frying pan and pour the beaten eggs and cook, drawing the egg mixture in from the sides of the pan until set on the bottom and creamy on top. Spoon the crab mixture down the center of the omelette and fold in half. Serve on a warm plate. Garnish with the coriander leaves and sprinkle with the peanuts. Serve with Savory Fish Sauce (see page 18).

Serves 4-6.

CRAB MEAT WITH CELLOPHANE NOODLES

2 tablespoons canola oil
3 cloves garlic, crushed
1 small yellow onion, finely chopped
1 cup canned crab meat
1 fresh, hot, red cayenne pepper, sliced (optional)
1 teaspoon sugar
3 tablespoons fish sauce
1/2 teaspoon ground white pepper
1 3 1/2 oz. pkg. cellophane noodles, soaked in warm water for 5 minutes, drained, cut into 2-inch lengths
4 green onions, chopped
1/4 cup fresh coriander leaves, chopped

Heat the oil in a wok over high heat and sauté the garlic and onion for 2 minutes or until light golden brown. Add the crab meat, cayenne pepper, sugar, fish sauce, pepper and cellophane noodles. Stir-fry for 3 minutes and garnish with the green onions and coriander leaves.

Serves 4-6.

CRAB MEAT WITH GINGER

2 tablespoons canola oil
2 tablespoons minced fresh
  ginger
4 green onions, chopped
2 cups canned crab meat
1/4 cup fish sauce
1/4 cup fresh coriander
  leaves, chopped

Heat the oil in a wok over medium heat and sauté the ginger and green onions for 1 minute. Add the crab meat and fish sauce and stir-fry for 2 minutes. Garnish with the coriander leaves.

Serves 4-6.

FISH CURRY WITH LEMON GRASS

1 stalk fresh lemon grass,
  finely minced
3 tablespoons curry powder
1/2 teaspoon salt
1 fresh, hot, red cayenne
  pepper, finely chopped
1/2 teaspoon ground white
  pepper
2 lbs. fillet of halibut
3 tablespoons canola oil
3 cloves garlic, crushed
1 small yellow onion, sliced
2 tablespoons fish sauce
1 tablespoon sugar
4 green onions, cut into
  2-inch lengths
1/4 cup fresh coriander
  leaves, chopped

In a bowl, thoroughly mix the lemon grass, curry powder, salt, cayenne pepper, and white pepper. Coat the fillet with this mixture. Marinate the fillet for at least 20 minutes or overnight in a refrigerator. Heat the oil in a large wok and fry the marinated fillet for 5 minutes on each side or until the fillet is cooked. Add the garlic, onion, fish sauce, sugar, and green onions. Simmer for 2 minutes and garnish with the coriander leaves.

Serves 4-6.

FISH WITH OYSTER SAUCE

1/2 teaspoon salt
1 tablespoon fish sauce
juice of 1 lime
1/2 teaspoon ground white
  pepper
2 lbs. fillet of flounder or
  sea bass
3 tablespoons canola oil
1 fresh, hot, red cayenne
  pepper, sliced (optional)
3 cloves garlic, crushed
1 small yellow onion, sliced
1 one-inch piece fresh
  ginger, cut into julienne
  strips
2 tablespoons oyster sauce
4 green onions, cut into
  2-inch lengths
1/4 cup fresh coriander
  leaves, chopped

In a large bowl, thoroughly mix the salt, fish sauce, lime juice, and white pepper. Add the fillet and marinate for at least 20 minutes or overnight in a refrigerator. Heat the oil in a large wok and fry the marinated fillet for 5 minutes on each side or until the fillet is cooked. Add the cayenne pepper, garlic, onion, ginger, oyster sauce, and green onions. Stir-fry for 1 minute and garnish with the coriander leaves.

Serves 4-6.

Fried Fish in Tomato Sauce

2 lbs. fillet of flounder or
  sea bass
1/2 teaspoon salt
1/4 cup canola oil
3 cloves garlic, crushed
3 green onions, cut into
  2-inch lengths
1/4 cup fish sauce
1 tablespoon sugar
1/2 teaspoon ground black
  pepper
2 large tomatoes, chopped
1/4 cup fresh coriander
  leaves, chopped

Place the flounder in a large bowl and rub it with salt. Set aside. Heat the oil in a large frying pan over a medium-high heat and fry the fillet for 5 minutes on each side or until the fillet is cooked. Remove to a warm plate. In the same frying pan with the remaining oil, stir-fry the garlic and green onions for 1 minute. Add the fish sauce, sugar, pepper and tomatoes. Simmer for 3 minutes, stirring frequently. Pour the sauce over the fillet and garnish with the coriander leaves.

Serves 4-6.

Fried Sweet and Sour Sauce

2 lbs. fillet of flounder
1/2 teaspoon salt
1/4 cup canola oil
3 cloves garlic, crushed
1 small yellow onion, thinly
   sliced
1 large carrot, peeled, cut
   into julienne strips
1/2 small white icicle radish,
   cut into julienne strips
2 tablespoons tomato paste
1/4 cup fish sauce
2 tablespoons sugar
juice of 1 lime
1/2 teaspoon ground white
   pepper
1/2 cup water
4 green onions, cut into
   2-inch lengths
1/4 cup fresh coriander
   leaves, chopped

Place the fillet in a large bowl, rub it with salt, and set it aside. Heat the oil in a frying pan over medium-high heat and fry the fillet for 5 minutes on each side or until the fillet is cooked. Remove to a warm plate. In the same frying pan with the remaining oil, stir-fry the garlic and onion until light golden brown. Add the carrot, white icicle radish and stir-fry for 2 minutes. Add the tomato paste, fish sauce, sugar, lime juice, pepper, water, and green onions. Simmer for 2 minutes, stirring frequently. Pour the sauce over the fillet and garnish with the coriander leaves.

Serves 4-6.

STEAMED SEA BASS

2 lbs. sea bass (Note: Any other white fish may be substituted.)
1/2 teaspoon salt
1 teaspoon sugar
1/2 teaspoon ground white pepper
2 tablespoons fish sauce
4 dried black Chinese mushrooms, soaked in 1/4 cup of warm water for 10 minutes (reserve the water), cut into julienne strips (Note: Discard the hard ends from the stems.)
2 green onions, cut into 2-inch lengths
3 cloves garlic, minced
1 one-inch piece fresh ginger, cut into julienne strips
1/4 cup fresh coriander leaves, chopped

Place the sea bass on a large oven-proof platter and sprinkle with the salt, sugar, pepper, and fish sauce. On top of the sea bass, arrange the black Chinese mushrooms, green onions, garlic, and ginger in layers. Pour the reserved, mushroom soaking water over the top of the fish. Place the fish platter onto the rack of a large steamer. Turn the temperature to medium-high heat and steam for 20 minutes or until the fish is cooked. Garnish with the coriander leaves. Serve warm over rice.

Serves 4-6.

Stuffed Baked Fish

1 whole sea bass or grouper
  (2-3 lbs.)
juice of 1 lime
1 teaspoon salt
1/4 lb. ground pork
4 green onions, chopped
4 cloves garlic, chopped
1 small yellow onion,
  chopped
1 teaspoon sugar
2 tablespoons dried black
  fungus strips, soaked in
  warm water for 3 minutes,
  drained, chopped
1 oz. cellophane noodles,
  soaked in warm water for 5
  minutes, drained, cut into
  2-inch lengths
1 egg yolk
1/2 teaspoon ground white
  pepper
1 fresh, hot, red cayenne
  pepper, cut into julienne
  strips (optional)
2 tablespoons canola oil
1/4 cup fresh coriander
  leaves, chopped

Place the fish in a large bowl and rub with the lime juice and salt. Set aside. In a small bowl, mix the pork, green onions, garlic, onion, sugar, black fungus, cellophane noodles, yolk, and white pepper. Stuff the fish with the pork mixture and place it on an oiled baking dish. Sprinkle the cayenne pepper and oil over the stuffed fish and bake in a 375 degree oven for 40 minutes or until the fish is cooked. Garnish with the coriander leaves.

Serves 4-6.

DRIED SHRIMP WITH TOFU

2 tablespoons canola oil
1 pkg. firm tofu (16 oz.),
  drained, cut into 1-inch
  cubes
3 cloves garlic, crushed
1/4 cup dried shrimp, soaked
  in 1/4 cup of warm water
  for 5 minutes, drained,
  (reserve the water),
  chopped
1/2 teaspoon salt
4 green onions, chopped
1/4 cup fresh coriander
  leaves, chopped

Heat the oil in a large wok and fry the tofu for 5 minutes or until golden brown on both sides. Add the garlic, shrimp with soaking water and salt and sauté for 2 minutes. Garnish with the green onions and coriander leaves.

Serves 4-6.

SAVORY SHRIMP

2 tablespoons canola oil
4 cloves garlic, crushed
2 lbs. large shrimp, shelled,
  deveined (see diagram,
  page 145)
1/4 cup fish sauce
1/2 teaspoon ground white
  pepper
2 tablespoons sugar
1 fresh, hot, red cayenne
  pepper, sliced (optional)
1/4 cup fresh coriander
  leaves, chopped

Heat the oil in a wok and sauté the garlic and shrimp for 3 minutes, stirring occasionally. Add the fish sauce, pepper, sugar, and cayenne pepper and continue to stir for 2 minutes. Garnish with the coriander leaves.

Serves 4-6.

SHRIMP CURRY

1 stalk fresh lemon grass, finely minced
3 tablespoons curry powder
2 tablespoons fish sauce
1 tablespoon brown sugar
2 lbs. shrimp, shelled, deveined (see diagram, page 145)
3 tablespoons canola oil
3 cloves garlic, crushed
1 small yellow onion, cut into 1-inch cubes
1 fresh, hot, red cayenne pepper, sliced
1 large carrot, peeled, thinly sliced
1 cup frozen green peas
1/2 teaspoon salt
1/2 teaspoon ground black pepper
1/4 cup fresh coriander leaves, chopped

In a bowl, thoroughly mix the lemon grass, curry powder, fish sauce, and sugar. Add the shrimp and marinate for at least 20 minutes or overnight in a refrigerator. Heat the oil in a large wok and stir-fry the garlic, onion, cayenne pepper, and marinated shrimp for 3 minutes, stirring occasionally. Add the carrot, green peas, salt, and pepper. Stir-fry for 2 minutes or until the shrimp is cooked. Do not overcook. Garnish with the coriander leaves. Serve warm over rice.

Serves 4-6.

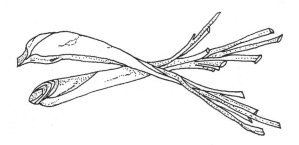

Shrimp with Garlic

2 lbs. shrimp, shelled,
deveined (see diagram,
page 145)
1 egg white, slightly beaten
2 tablespoons cornstarch
1/2 teaspoon salt
1/2 teaspoon ground white
pepper
6 cloves garlic, minced
3 tablespoons canola oil
1 small yellow onion, sliced
1 stalk fresh lemon grass,
cut into 2-inch lengths
1 fresh, hot, red cayenne
pepper, sliced (optional)
4 green onions, cut into
2-inch lengths
1 tablespoon fish sauce
1/4 cup fresh coriander
leaves, chopped

In a bowl, thoroughly mix the shrimp, egg white, cornstarch, salt, pepper, and garlic. Marinate the shrimp for at least 15 minutes or overnight in a refrigerator. Heat the oil in a large wok and sauté the onion for 1 minute. Add the lemon grass, cayenne pepper, and marinated shrimp. Stir-fry for 3 minutes, stirring occasionally, until the shrimp is cooked. Do not overcook. Add the green onions and fish sauce and stir-fry for 2 minutes. Garnish with the coriander leaves.

Serves 4-6.

SHRIMP WITH SNOW PEAS

1 lb. shrimp, shelled, deveined (see diagram, page 145)
1 egg white slightly beaten
2 tablespoons cornstarch
1 tablespoon fish sauce
1 teaspoon brown sugar
1/2 teaspoon ground white pepper
3 tablespoons canola oil
4 cloves garlic, crushed
1 small yellow onion, sliced
1 lb. snow peas, ends removed, washed
2 tablespoons oyster sauce

In a bowl, thoroughly mix the shrimp, egg white, cornstarch, fish sauce, sugar, and pepper. Marinate the shrimp for at least 15 minutes or overnight in a refrigerator. Heat the oil in a large wok and stir-fry the garlic and onion for 1 minute. Add the marinated shrimp and stir-fry for 3 minutes, stirring occasionally, until the shrimp is cooked. Do not overcook. Add the snow peas and oyster sauce and stir-fry for 2 minutes. Serve warm over rice.

Serves 4-6.

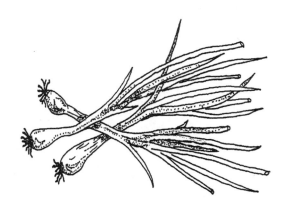

SHRIMP WITH VEGETABLES

1 lb. large shrimp, shelled,
  deveined (see diagram,
  page 145)
3 cloves garlic, crushed
1 tablespoon fish sauce
1/2 teaspoon ground white
  pepper
1 tablespoon cornstarch
3 tablespoons canola oil
1 tablespoon sesame oil
1 one-inch piece fresh
  ginger, cut into julienne
  strips
1 carrot, peeled, thinly sliced
1 cup fresh mushrooms,
  washed, drained, sliced
1 small yellow onion, sliced
1 small zucchini, thinly
  sliced
1 teaspoon salt
4 green onions, cut into
  2-inch lengths

In a small bowl, marinate the shrimp with garlic, fish sauce, pepper, and cornstarch for 5 minutes in a refrigerator. Heat the canola oil in a large wok, sauté the shrimp for 3 minutes, stirring occasionally, until the shrimp is cooked. Do not overcook. Remove and set aside. In the same wok, heat the sesame oil and stir-fry the ginger, carrot, mushrooms, onion, and zucchini for 2 minutes or until the vegetables are cooked. Do not overcook. Add the sautéed shrimp, salt, and green onions and stir-fry for 1 minute. Serve warm over rice.

Serves 4-6.

SWEET AND SOUR SHRIMP

2 lbs. large shrimp, shelled, deveined (see diagram, page 145)
1 tablespoon fish sauce
1 egg white, beaten
1/2 teaspoon ground white pepper
3 cloves garlic, crushed
2 tablespoons cornstarch
3 tablespoons canola oil
1 tablespoon sesame oil
1/4 cup dried black fungus strips, soaked in warm water for 3 minutes, drained
1/2 cup frozen green peas
1 small carrot, peeled, thinly sliced
2 tablespoons ketchup
1 teaspoon salt
juice of 1 lime
2 tablespoons sugar
2 green onions, chopped

In a large bowl, marinate the shrimp with fish sauce, egg white, pepper, garlic, and cornstarch for 5 minutes in a refrigerator. Heat the canola oil in a large wok and sauté the shrimp for 3 minutes, stirring occasionally, until the shrimp is cooked. Do not overcook. Remove and set aside. In the same wok, heat the sesame oil and stir-fry the black fungus, green peas, and carrot for 2 minutes. Add the ketchup, salt, lime juice, sugar and sautéed shrimp and stir-fry for 1 minute. Garnish with the green onions.

Serves 4-6.

STUFFED SQUID WITH PORK

1 lb. squid, cleaned
(see diagram, page 143)
4 dried black Chinese
mushrooms, soaked in 1/4
cup of warm water for 10
minutes (remove the hard
ends from the stems), cut
into julienne strips
10 dried lily buds, soaked in
1/4 cup warm water for 10
minutes (Note: Discard the
hard ends from the stems
and the soaking water.)
1/2 lb. lean ground pork
1/2 cup cellophane noodles,
soaked, drained, cut into
4-inch lengths
3 cloves garlic, minced
4 green onions, chopped
1/4 teaspoon ground white
pepper
1/2 teaspoon salt
1 tablespoon fish sauce
1 cup canola oil

Clean the squid thoroughly, discarding the head and everything inside the body. Reserve tentacles. Peel off the outer skin and rinse the body, inside and out. Drain in a colander for about 3 minutes. Chop the tentacles finely. In a small bowl, thoroughly mix the black Chinese mushrooms, lily buds, ground pork, cellophane noodles, garlic, green onions, pepper, salt, fish sauce, and chopped tentacles. Stuff the pork mixture into the squid, packing it firmly. Close the opening of the stuffed squid with a toothpick. Heat the oil in a wok and deep-fry the stuffed squid for 15 minutes on each side or until the stuffed squid is thoroughly cooked. Serve with Mixed Vegetable Pickles (see page 13), and Savory Fish Sauce (see page 18).

Serves 4-6.

CHAPTER SEVEN

MEAT
&
POULTRY

Meat and Poultry

Barbecued Beef Wrapped in Rice Papers

2 stalks fresh lemon grass, chopped
3 cloves garlic, crushed
1 small yellow onion, chopped
1 tablespoon sugar
3 tablespoons fish sauce
1/2 teaspoon ground white pepper
2 lbs. tenderloin beef, thinly sliced
1 tablespoon sesame oil
1 tablespoon sesame seeds
6" bamboo skewers, soaked in water for 15 minutes, drained
20 sheets dried rice papers (Before wrapping, soak them one by one under the water for 2 minutes or until softened.)
2 cups fresh mint leaves
2 cups fresh coriander leaves
1 cup Green Onion with Oil (see page 15)

In a blender, blend the lemon grass, garlic, onion, sugar, fish sauce, and pepper into a smooth sauce. Pour the sauce into a large bowl and add the sliced beef and sesame seeds. Mix well and marinate the beef for at least 1 hour or overnight in a refrigerator. Put 4 pieces of beef on each skewer and broil over a hot charcoal fire until cooked throughout, or in the oven for 3 minutes on each side. To serve, place each soaked rice paper on a plate and put a small piece of beef or two, a few mint leaves, a few coriander leaves, and 1 teaspoon of Green Onion with Oil on it. Roll it into a cylinder shape. After finishing all 20 sheets of rice papers, arrange them on a large platter. Serve with Savory Fish Sauce (see page 18) or Sweet and Spicy Sauce (see page 20).

Serves 4-6.

COCONUT SODA BEEF WITH LEMON GRASS

2 lbs. top sirloin, cut into
  2-inch cubes
3 tablespoons curry powder
1 teaspoon sugar
1 teaspoon salt
3 cloves garlic, crushed
1/2 teaspoon ground black
  pepper
2 tablespoons canola oil
1 tablespoon tomato paste
4 bay laurel leaves
2 stalks fresh lemon grass,
  cut into 2-inch lengths
6 cups water
2 large carrots, peeled, cut
  into 1-inch lengths
1 can coconut soda (soft
  drink) (12 fl. oz.)
2 large potatoes, peeled, cut
  into 4 wedges
1/4 cup fresh coriander
  leaves, chopped

In a large bowl, thoroughly mix the beef, curry powder, sugar, salt, garlic, and pepper. Marinate the beef for at least 1 hour or overnight in a refrigerator. Heat the oil in a large deep pot and stir-fry the beef for 2 minutes or until light golden brown. Add the tomato paste, bay laurel leaves, lemon grass, and water. Cover and simmer for 1 hour or until the beef is tender. Add the carrots and coconut soda and simmer for 10 minutes. Add the potatoes and simmer for 15 minutes. Garnish with the coriander leaves. Serve with French bread or rice.

Serves 4-6.

GINGER BEEF WITH ONIONS

3 tablespoons canola oil
3 cloves garlic, crushed
1 one-inch piece fresh
  ginger, cut into julienne
  strips
1 lb. top sirloin beef, thinly
  sliced, coated on both
  sides with 1 tablespoon
  of cornstarch
2 tablespoons fish sauce
1 teaspoon sugar
1 large yellow onion, thinly
  sliced
1/4 cup fresh coriander
  leaves, chopped

Heat the oil in a wok and sauté the garlic and ginger until light golden brown. Add the beef, fish sauce, sugar, and onion and stir-fry for 3 minutes, stirring occasionally. Garnish with the coriander leaves.

Serves 4.

GROUND BEEF WITH LEMON GRASS

2 tablespoon canola oil
1 stalk lemon grass, finely
  chopped
4 cloves garlic, crushed
1 small yellow onion, finely
  chopped
2 lbs. extra lean ground beef
3 tablespoons fish sauce
1 teaspoon sugar
1/2 teaspoon ground white
  pepper
1/4 cup fresh coriander
  leaves, chopped

Heat the oil in a wok and sauté the lemon grass, garlic, and onion until light golden brown. Add the beef and stir-fry for 5 minutes, stirring occasionally. Add the fish sauce, sugar, and pepper and stir-fry for 3 more minutes. Garnish with the coriander leaves. Serve warm over rice.

Serves 4-6.

STIR-FRIED BEEF WITH BAMBOO SHOOTS

2 tablespoons canola oil
3 cloves garlic, crushed
1 large yellow onion, sliced
1 lb. tenderloin beef, thinly
  sliced
1 cup canned bamboo
  shoots, thinly sliced
3 tablespoons fish sauce
1 fresh red cayenne pepper,
  sliced
1 teaspoon sugar
1/2 teaspoon ground white
  pepper
2 tablespoons cornstarch,
  dissolved in a 1/4 cup of
  cold water
1/4 cup fresh coriander
  leaves, chopped

Heat the oil in a large frying pan and stir-fry the garlic and onion until light golden brown. Add the beef, bamboo shoots, fish sauce, cayenne pepper, sugar, and pepper and stir-fry for 3 minutes, stirring occasionally. Add the cornstarch mixture and stir-fry for 2 minutes, stirring frequently. Garnish with the coriander leaves. Serve warm over rice.

Serves 4.

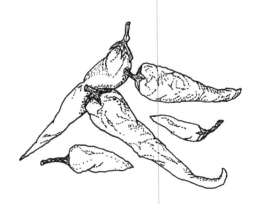

STIR-FRIED BEEF WITH BROCCOLI

1 lb. top sirloin, thinly sliced
2 tablespoons fish sauce
3 cloves garlic, crushed
1/2 teaspoon ground black
  pepper
1 teaspoon sugar
1 tablespoon soy sauce
2 tablespoons cornstarch
1/4 cup canola oil
1 lb. fresh broccoli, cut into
  small florets (discard the
  tough stems)
1 tablespoon oyster sauce

In a small bowl, thoroughly mix the beef, fish sauce, garlic, pepper, sugar, soy sauce, and cornstarch. Marinate the beef for at least 20 minutes or overnight in a refrigerator. Heat the oil in a wok and sauté the beef for 3 minutes or until the beef is cooked. Place the beef on a plate and set aside. Using the same wok, stir-fry the broccoli for 2 minutes; then, cover it for an additional minute. Add the sautéed beef and oyster sauce and mix well. Serve warm over rice.

Serves 4-6.

STIR-FRIED BEEF WITH CELERY

1 lb. top sirloin, thinly sliced
2 tablespoons fish sauce
3 cloves garlic, crushed
1/2 teaspoon ground white
  pepper
2 tablespoons cornstarch
3 tablespoons canola oil
1 large carrot, peeled, cut
  into julienne strips
2 stalks celery with leaves,
  cut into 2-inch julienne
  strips
1 green bell pepper, seeded,
  thinly sliced
1 red bell pepper, seeded,
  thinly sliced
1 small yellow onion, thinly
  sliced
1 teaspoon sugar
1 teaspoon salt
1/4 cup fresh coriander
  leaves, chopped

In a small bowl, thoroughly mix the beef, fish sauce, garlic, pepper, and cornstarch. Marinate the beef for at least 20 minutes or overnight in a refrigerator. Heat 2 tablespoons of oil in a wok and sauté the beef for 3 minutes, stirring occasionally. Place the beef on a plate and set aside. Using the same wok, add 1 tablespoon of oil and stir-fry the carrot and celery for 2 minutes. Add the green bell pepper, red bell pepper, onion, sugar, and salt and stir-fry for 2 minutes. Add the sautéed beef and stir-fry for 1 minute. Transfer to a serving platter and garnish with the coriander leaves. Serve hot over rice.

Serves 4-6.

STIR-FRIED BEEF WITH GREEN BEANS

1 lb. top sirloin beef, thinly sliced
2 tablespoons soy sauce
3 cloves garlic, crushed
1/2 teaspoon ground white pepper
1 tablespoon cornstarch
1/2 teaspoon salt
1 teaspoon sugar
1 teaspoon sesame oil
3 tablespoons canola oil
1 small yellow onion, sliced
1 lb. string beans, ends removed, cut into 1-inch lengths
1 tablespoon oyster sauce (optional)

In a large bowl, thoroughly mix the sliced beef, soy sauce, garlic, pepper, cornstarch, salt, sugar, and sesame oil. Marinate the beef for at least 15 minutes or overnight in a refrigerator. In a wok, heat 2 tablespoons of oil and sauté the beef for 2 minutes, stirring occasionally. Place on a platter and set aside. Heat 1 tablespoon of oil in another wok and stir-fry the onion and string beans for 2 minutes. Add the oyster sauce and cover. Reduce the heat to low and simmer for 3 minutes or until the beans are crispy tender. Uncover and add the sautéed beef and mix well. Serve over rice. The same recipe can be used for tofu, celery with carrots, broccoli, or cauliflower in place of the string beans.

Serves 4-6.

STIR-FRIED BEEF WITH LEMON GRASS

1 lb. beef tenderloin, thinly sliced
1 stalk fresh lemon grass, minced
4 cloves garlic, crushed
2 tablespoons fish sauce
1 tablespoon ground allspice
1 teaspoon sugar
1/2 teaspoon ground white pepper
3 tablespoons canola oil
1 large yellow onion, sliced
1/4 cup roasted peanuts, chopped
1/4 cup fresh coriander leaves, chopped

In a small bowl, thoroughly mix the beef, lemon grass, garlic, fish sauce, allspice, sugar, and pepper. Marinate the beef for at least 1 hour or overnight in a refrigerator. Heat the oil in a large frying pan and sauté the beef and onion for 3 minutes, stirring occasionally. Sprinkle with the peanuts and garnish with the coriander leaves.

Serves 4.

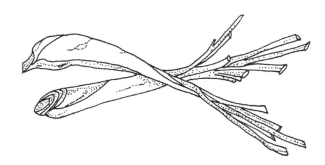

BAKED GROUND PORK CASSEROLE

1 3 1/2 oz. pkg. cellophane noodles, soaked in warm water for 5 minutes, drained, cut into 2-inch lengths

1/4 cup dried black fungus strips, soaked in warm water for 3 minutes, drained, chopped

2 green onions, chopped

1 small yellow onion, finely chopped

2 lbs. lean ground pork

3 tablespoons fish sauce

1/2 teaspoon ground white pepper

1 teaspoon sugar

3 eggs, beaten

In a large bowl, thoroughly mix the cellophane noodles, black fungus strips, green onions, onion, pork, fish sauce, pepper, sugar, and eggs. Pour into an oiled 9x13 inch baking pan and press the mixture flat. Bake in a 350 degree oven for 40 minutes or until done. Let cool before cutting into small squares. Serve with Savory Fish Sauce (see page 18).

Serves 4-6.

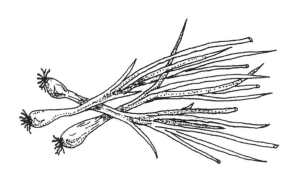

BARBECUED PORK

4 cloves garlic, crushed
1/4 cup light soy sauce
2 tablespoons cooking wine
2 tablespoons sugar
2 green onions, cut into
2-inch lengths
2 slices ginger
6 star aniseeds
1 teaspoon Chinese five
spice powder
4 lb. pork roast

In a large bowl, mix the garlic, soy sauce, wine, sugar, green onions, ginger, star aniseeds, and five spice powder. Add the pork and marinate for at least 1 hour or overnight in a refrigerator. Place the pork in a large roasting pan and pour the mixture over it. Bake covered, about 40 minutes, in a preheated oven at 350 degrees. Uncover and bake for 20 minutes or until the pork is tender and the top is golden brown. Let cool before slicing into small pieces. Serve with Plum Sauce (see page 17).

Serves 4-6.

Barbecued Pork Chops

2 stalks fresh lemon grass, chopped
4 cloves garlic, crushed
1 large white onion, sliced
1 tablespoon brown sugar
2 fresh, hot, red cayenne peppers, sliced (optional)
juice of 1 lime
3 tablespoons fish sauce
1/2 teaspoon ground white pepper
1/2 cup roasted peanuts, finely chopped
2 lbs. thinly sliced pork chops
1/4 cup fresh coriander leaves, chopped
1 cup Green Onion with Oil (see page 15)

In a blender, blend the lemon grass, garlic, onion, brown sugar, cayenne peppers, lime juice, fish sauce, and pepper into a smooth sauce. Pour the lemon grass sauce into a large bowl and add the peanuts and pork chops. Mix and marinate the pork chops for at least 1 hour or overnight in a refrigerator. Broil the pork chops over a hot charcoal fire until cooked thoroughout, or broil them in the oven for 3 minutes on each side, turning occasionally, or until pork chops are cooked. Garnish with the coriander leaves and Green Onion with Oil. Serve with Mixed Vegetable Pickles (see page 13), Lime Sauce (see page 16) or Savory Fish Sauce (see page 18).

Serves 4-6.

FIVE SPICES PORK WITH EGGS

2 tablespoons canola oil
4 cloves garlic, crushed
2 lb. pork shoulder, cut into
2-inch cubes
2 shallots, peeled
1 tablespoon sugar
2 tablespoons fish sauce
1 tablespoon light soy sauce
1 tablespoon five spice
powder
1/2 teaspoon ground black
pepper
4 cups water
6 hard-boiled eggs, shelled
(optional)
1/4 cup fresh coriander
leaves, chopped

Heat the oil in a large deep pot and stir-fry the garlic and pork until golden brown on both sides. Add the shallots, sugar, fish sauce, soy sauce, five spice powder, pepper, and water. Simmer for 1 hour or until the pork is tender. Add the hard-boiled eggs and simmer for 20 minutes. Garnish with the coriander leaves. Serve hot over rice.

Serves 4-6.

Pork Chops with Tomato Sauce

2 tablespoons canola oil
4 cloves garlic, crushed
2 lbs. pork chops
2 tablespoons fish sauce
1/4 cup light soy sauce
2 tablespoons tomato paste
1 cup water
2 tablespoons sugar
1/4 cup fresh coriander
  leaves, chopped

Heat the oil in a large frying pan and sauté the garlic and pork chops for 3 minutes or until golden brown on both sides. Add the fish sauce, soy sauce, tomato paste, water, and sugar. Simmer for 30 minutes or until the pork is tender and the sauce is thick. Garnish with the coriander leaves. Serve warm over rice.

Serves 4-6.

Pork with Lemon Grass

4 cups water
2 lb. pork shoulder, cut into
  1-inch thick slices
2 stalks fresh lemon grass,
  cut into 2-inch lengths
1 cup roasted peanuts,
  shelled
1 tablespoon curry powder
1 teaspoon salt
1 tablespoon sugar

Bring the water to a boil in a deep pot and add the pork and lemon grass. Cook over medium-low heat for 1 hour or until the pork is tender. Add the peanuts, curry powder, salt, and sugar. Simmer for 10 minutes. Serve over rice.

Serves 4-6.

PORK WITH SHRIMP

1/4 cup canola oil for deep-frying

1 pkg. firm tofu (16 oz.), drained, cubed

1/2 lb. tenderloin pork, thinly sliced

1/2 lb. large shrimp, shelled, deveined (see diagram, page 145)

3 cloves garlic, crushed

1/2 teaspoon ground white pepper

2 tablespoons fish sauce

3 tablespoons cornstarch

3 tablespoons canola oil

1 one-inch piece fresh ginger, cut into julienne strips

1 fresh, hot, red cayenne pepper, sliced (optional)

1 large white onion, thinly sliced

1 tablespoon brown sugar

1 tablespoon oyster sauce

4 green onions, cut into 2-inch lengths

1/4 cup fresh coriander leaves, chopped

Heat the oil in a large frying pan and deep-fry the tofu until golden brown on both sides. Remove and drain on paper towels. Set aside. In a small bowl, thoroughly mix the pork, shrimp, garlic, white pepper, fish sauce, and cornstarch. Heat the oil in a wok and stir-fry the coated pork and shrimp for 3 minutes, stirring occasionally. Add the fried tofu, ginger, cayenne pepper, onion, brown sugar, oyster sauce, and green onions. Stir-fry for 2 minutes, stirring frequently, or until the pork and shrimp are cooked. Do not overcook. Garnish with the coriander leaves.

Serves 4-6.

STEAMED GROUND PORK WITH EGGS

1 tablespoon canola oil
4 dried black Chinese
   mushrooms, soaked in
   1/4 cup of warm water for
   15 minutes (reserve the
   water), cut into julienne
   strips (Note: Discard the
   hard ends from the
   stems.)
1/2 teaspoon salt
1 tablespoon fish sauce
1/4 cup water
1/2 teaspoon ground white
   pepper
4 eggs, beaten
1 lb. lean ground pork
4 green onions, chopped
1/4 cup fresh coriander
   leaves, chopped

Heat the oil in a small pot and sauté the mushrooms and salt for 1 minute. Place the sautéed mushrooms in a large bowl with the reserved mushroom soaking water, fish sauce, water, pepper, eggs, ground pork, and green onions. Thoroughly mix and pour the mixture into a large casserole. Place the casserole into a bamboo steamer and cover. Steam for 40 minutes or until the eggs are set. Garnish with the coriander leaves. Serve warm over rice.

Serves 4-6.

Stir-Fried Tofu with Ground Pork

2 tablespoons canola oil
1 pkg. firm tofu (16 oz.),
  drained, cubed
3 cloves garlic, crushed
1/2 lb. lean ground pork
1/2 teaspoon ground white
  pepper
2 tablespoons light soy
  sauce
2 tablespoons of cornstarch
  dissolved in 1/4 cup of
  water
1 tablespoon soy bean
  paste (Brown Rice Miso),
  dissolved in 1/4 cup of
   warm water
1 tablespoon sugar
1 fresh, hot, red cayenne
  pepper, sliced (optional)
4 green onions, chopped
2 tablespoons fresh
  coriander leaves
2 tablespoons sesame oil

Heat the oil in a large wok and fry the tofu for 2 minutes or until golden brown on both sides. Add the garlic, pork, and pepper and sauté for 3 minutes, stirring occasionally. Add the soy sauce, cornstarch mixture, soy bean paste, sugar, and cayenne pepper and simmer for 2 minutes, stirring frequently. Garnish with the green onions and coriander leaves. Sprinkle with the sesame oil. Serve warm over rice.

Serves 4-6.

Stuffed Tofu with Ground Pork

1 pkg. extra firm tofu
 (12.4 oz.), drained
1/4 lb. lean ground pork
3 cloves garlic, crushed
2 green onions, finely
 chopped
1/2 teaspoon ground white
 pepper
2 tablespoons fish sauce
1 tablespoon cornstarch
1 egg, beaten
3 tablespoons canola oil
1 cup water
1 tablespoon sugar
1 tablespoon light soy sauce
1/2 teaspoon salt
1 tablespoon tomato paste
1/4 cup fresh coriander
 leaves, chopped

Cut the tofu into 2-inch cubes and scoop out the center of each cube. Set aside the outer tofu shells. In a large bowl, mix the scooped out tofu, pork, garlic, green onions, pepper, fish sauce, cornstarch, and egg. Stuff the tofu cubes with this mixture. Heat the oil in a large wok and fry the stuffed tofu for 3 minutes on each side or until golden brown on both sides. Add the water, sugar, soy sauce, salt, and tomato paste. Stir and simmer for 20 minutes or until the stuffed tofu is cooked. Garnish with the coriander leaves. Serve warm over rice.

Serves 4-6.

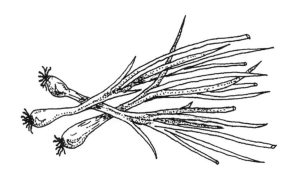

TOMATOES STUFFED WITH GROUND PORK

6 firm medium-sized red
  tomatoes
1/2 lb. lean ground pork
2 green onions, chopped
3 cloves garlic, crushed
1 small yellow onion, finely
  chopped
1/4 teaspoon salt
2 tablespoons fish sauce
1 teaspoon sugar
1 tablespoon cornstarch
1/2 teaspoon ground white
  pepper
2 tablespoons canola oil
1/4 cup fresh coriander
  leaves, chopped

Cut the tops off the tomatoes, remove the pulp with a spoon, and discard the tops and pulp. In a small bowl, thoroughly mix the ground pork, green onions, garlic, onion, salt, fish sauce, sugar, cornstarch and white pepper. Dry the insides of the tomatoes with a paper towel. (It is important that they be dry to prevent the mixture falling out.) Stuff the tomatoes with the pork mixture, pressing it in firmly. Heat the oil over medium-high heat in a large frying pan and place the tomatoes, meat side down, into the frying pan. Cover and turn the heat down to medium and cook for 6 minutes. Turn the tomatoes, meat side up, and cook covered for another 3 minutes. Garnish with the coriander leaves.

Serves 4-6.

BARBECUED CHICKEN WITH LEMON GRASS

1 stalk lemon grass,
  chopped
1 large yellow onion, sliced
3 cloves garlic, crushed
1 tablespoon sugar
1/4 cup fish sauce
3 lb. whole chicken, cut
  into small pieces
1/4 cup roasted peanuts,
  chopped

In a blender, blend the lemon grass, onion, garlic, and sugar into a paste. Pour the mixture in a large bowl and add the chicken pieces. Mix and marinate the chicken pieces for at least 1 hour or overnight in a refrigerator. Broil over a hot charcoal fire until cooked throughout, or in a broiler for 20 minutes on each side, turning frequently to avoid burning the meat. Sprinkle with the peanuts. Serve with Lime Sauce (see page 16), or Savory Fish Sauce (see page 18).

Serves 4-6.

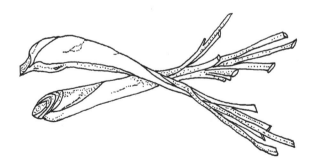

CHICKEN CURRY

3 lb. whole chicken, cut into
small pieces
2 large potatoes, peeled, cut
into 2-inch cubes
1 tablespoon fish sauce
4 cloves garlic, crushed
1 teaspoon salt
1/4 cup curry powder
1/4 cup canola oil
1 large yellow onion, cut into
4 wedges
1 stalk fresh lemon grass,
cut into 2-inch lengths
3 bay leaves
4 cups water
3 large carrots, peeled,
sliced
1 can coconut milk
(14 fl. oz.)
1 loaf French bread, sliced

In a large bowl, thoroughly mix the chicken pieces, potatoes, fish sauce, garlic, salt, and curry powder. Marinate the chicken pieces for at least 1 hour or overnight in a refrigerator. Heat the oil in a large frying pan and fry the chicken pieces and potatoes until golden brown on both sides. Place the fried chicken pieces and fried potatoes in a large pot with the onion, lemon grass, bay leaves, and water. Cook for 30 minutes or until the chicken pieces are cooked. Add the carrots and simmer for 15 minutes. Add the coconut milk, stir, and simmer for 5 minutes. Serve with French bread or over rice.

Serves 4-6.

CHICKEN WITH LEMON GRASS

2 stalks fresh lemon grass,
  chopped
1 large white onion, sliced
1 fresh, hot, red cayenne
  pepper, sliced
4 cloves garlic, crushed
1 tablespoon brown sugar
3 tablespoons fish sauce
1/2 teaspoon ground white
  pepper
2 lbs. boneless chicken
  breasts, skinned
3 tablespoons canola oil
juice of 1 lime
1/4 cup roasted peanuts,
  chopped
1/4 cup fresh coriander
  leaves, chopped

In a blender, blend the lemon grass, onion, cayenne pepper, garlic, sugar, fish sauce, and pepper into a smooth sauce. Pour the lemon grass sauce into a large bowl and marinate the chicken breasts for at least 1 hour or overnight in a refrigerator. Heat the oil in a large frying pan and fry the marinated chicken breasts over medium-low heat for 15 minutes on each side, turning occasionally, or until the chicken is cooked and no longer looks pink. Sprinkle with lime juice and peanuts. Garnish with the coriander leaves. Serve with Savory Fish Sauce (see page 18).

Serves 4-6.

GINGER CHICKEN

2 tablespoons canola oil
3 cloves garlic, crushed
1/2-inch piece fresh ginger,
   thinly sliced
1 large yellow onion, finely
   chopped
4 lbs. drumsticks
1/2 teaspoon ground white
   pepper
1 tablespoon brown sugar
1/4 cup fish sauce
2 fresh, hot, red cayenne
   peppers, sliced (optional)
4 green onions, cut into
   2-inch lengths

Heat the oil in a large deep pot and stir-fry the garlic, ginger, onion and drumsticks for 2 minutes. Add the pepper, sugar, fish sauce and cayenne peppers. Cook for 40 minutes or until the drumsticks are cooked. Garnish with the green onions. Serve with the Ginger Fish Sauce (see page 15).

Serves 6-8.

Spicy Ground Chicken

1/4 cup canola oil
2 lbs. ground chicken
1 stalk fresh lemon grass, finely chopped
4 cloves garlic, crushed
1/4 cup fish sauce
1 tablespoon sugar
1/2 teaspoon ground black pepper
2 fresh, hot, red cayenne peppers, finely chopped
1/2 teaspoon salt
1/4 cup fresh coriander leaves, chopped
4 green onions, chopped

Heat the oil in a wok and stir-fry the chicken, lemon grass, and garlic for 10 minutes, stirring occasionally, or until the chicken is cooked. Add the fish sauce, sugar, pepper, cayenne peppers, and salt. Simmer for 5 minutes and garnish with the coriander leaves and green onions. Serve over rice.

Serves 4-6.

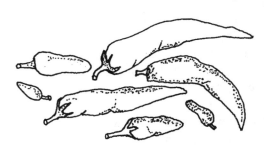

STEAMED CHICKEN WITH GINGER

1 lb. boneless chicken
   breasts, skinned, thinly
   sliced
1/2 lb. boneless chicken
   thighs, skinned, thinly
   sliced
1/2 teaspoon salt
2 large red tomatoes,
   chopped
3 cloves garlic, crushed
4 dried black Chinese
   mushrooms, soaked
   in 1/4 cup of warm water
   for 10 minutes (reserve
   the water), cut into
   julienne strips. (Note:
   Remove the hard ends
   from the stems.)
1 one-inch piece fresh
   ginger, cut into julienne
   strips
3 tablespoons fish sauce
1 teaspoon brown sugar
1/2 teaspoon ground white
   pepper
4 green onions, cut into
   2-inch lengths
1 fresh, hot, red cayenne
   pepper, sliced (optional)
1/4 cup fresh coriander
   leaves, chopped

In a large heat-proof bowl, arrange the sliced chicken breasts, chicken thighs, salt, tomatoes, garlic, and black Chinese mushrooms in layers. In a small bowl, combine the reserved mushroom soaking water, ginger, fish sauce, brown sugar, pepper, green onions, and cayenne pepper. Pour the mixture over the layered chicken and vegetables. Place in a steamer and cook for 30-35 minutes or until chicken is tender. Garnish with the coriander leaves.

Serves 4-6.

Stir-Fried Chicken with Broccoli

1 whole boneless chicken breast, skinned, thinly sliced
3 cloves garlic, crushed
1/2 teaspoon ground black pepper
2 tablespoons fish sauce
2 tablespoons cornstarch
1/4 cup canola oil
1 small yellow onion, cut into 4 wedges
2 lbs. fresh broccoli, cut into small florets (discard the tough stems)
1/4 cup oyster sauce

In a small bowl, marinate the sliced chicken with garlic, pepper, and fish sauce for 5 minutes in a refrigerator. Coat the marinated chicken with cornstarch. Heat 2 tablespoons of oil in a wok and sauté the coated chicken for 3 minutes, stirring occasionally. Remove and set aside. In the same wok, heat the remaining oil over high heat. Add the onion and broccoli and stir-fry for 2 minutes, stirring frequently. Reduce the heat to low and cover for 3 minutes. Uncover and add the sautéed chicken and oyster sauce and stir for 1 minute. Serve hot over rice.

Serves 4-6.

STIR-FRIED CHICKEN WITH STRING BEANS

2 tablespoons canola oil

3 cloves garlic, crushed

1 lb. boneless chicken breasts, thinly sliced

1 lb. fresh string beans, ends removed, cut into 2-inch lengths

1 cup canned bamboo shoots, cut into julienne strips

2 dried black Chinese mushrooms, soaked in 1/4 cup of warm water for 10 minutes (reserve the water), cut into julienne strips (Note: Remove the hard ends from the stems.)

2 green onions, cut into 2-inch lengths

1 tablespoon white cooking wine

1 tablespoon soy sauce

1 teaspoon salt

1 teaspoon sugar (optional)

1/4 cup fresh coriander leaves, chopped

Heat the oil in a wok and stir-fry the garlic and chicken for 3 minutes, stirring frequently. Add the string beans, bamboo shoots, black Chinese mushrooms, reserved mushroom soaking water, green onions, wine, soy sauce, salt, and sugar. Simmer for 5 minutes and garnish with the coriander leaves. Serve warm over rice.

Serves 4-6.

CHAPTER EIGHT

RICE
&
NOODLES

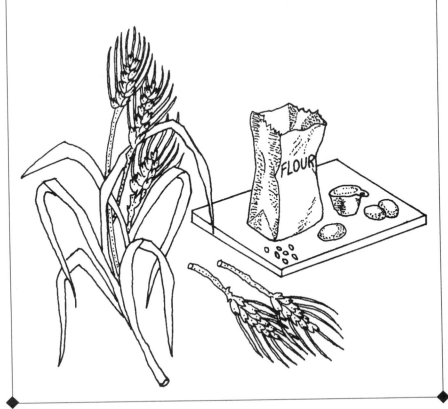

CHAPTER EIGHT
Rice and Noodles

GLUTINOUS RICE

**2 cups glutinous rice,
washed, drained
1/4 teaspoon salt
2 1/2 cups water**

In a large, uncovered pot, bring the rice, salt, and water to a boil over high heat for 3 minutes, stirring occasionally. Reduce the heat to low and cover the pot. Simmer for 30 minutes or until the rice is soft. Remove and serve warm.

Serves 4-6.

LONG-GRAIN WHITE RICE

**2 cups long-grain rice,
washed, drained
3 cups water
1/4 teaspoon salt**

In a large, uncovered pot, bring the rice, water and salt to a boil over high heat for 3 minutes, stirring occasionally. Reduce the heat to low and cover the pot. Simmer for 20 minutes or until the rice is soft. Remove and serve warm.

Serves 4-6.

STIR-FRIED RICE WITH PORK

2 tablespoons canola oil
1 small yellow onion,
   chopped
3 cloves garlic, crushed
1/2 lb. pork loin or chicken
   breasts, cut into julienne
   strips
1 carrot, peeled, chopped
1/2 teaspoon salt
1/2 teaspoon ground white
   pepper
3 cups cooked long-grain
   rice (see page 129)
2 tablespoons fish sauce
   or light soy sauce
1 cup frozen peas
4 green onions, chopped
1/4 cup fresh coriander
   leaves, chopped

Heat the oil in a large wok and stir-fry the onion and garlic until light golden brown. Add the pork and carrot and stir-fry for 5 minutes, stirring frequently. Add the salt, pepper, rice, fish sauce, and frozen peas. Stir well for 2 minutes. Transfer to a large serving platter and garnish with the green onions and coriander leaves. The same recipe can be used with shrimp or scrambled eggs.

Serves 4-6.

STIR-FRIED RICE WITH SHRIMP

2 tablespoons canola oil
1 small yellow onion, finely
   chopped
4 cloves garlic, crushed
1/2 lb. shrimp, shelled,
   deveined (see diagram,
   page 145)
1/2 cup canned crab meat
4 cups cooked long-grain
   white rice (see page 129)
1/2 teaspoon salt
1/2 teaspoon ground white
   pepper
2 tablespoons fish sauce
4 green onions, chopped
1/4 cup fresh coriander
   leaves, chopped

Heat the oil in a large wok and stir-fry the onion and garlic for 2 minutes or until light golden brown. Add the shrimp and stir-fry for 3 minutes, stirring frequently. Add the crab meat, rice, salt, pepper, and fish sauce. Stir well for 2 minutes. Garnish with the green onions and coriander leaves.

Serves 4-6.

CHICKEN CHOW MEIN

2 tablespoons canola oil
3 cloves garlic, crushed
1 small yellow onion, chopped
1 lb. boneless chicken breasts, thinly sliced
2 large carrots, peeled, cut into julienne strips
1 small green cabbage, cut into 1-inch squares
1/4 cup oyster sauce
1/2 teaspoon ground white pepper
4 green onions, cut into 1-inch lengths
1 lb. cooked egg noodles
1/4 cup fresh coriander leaves, chopped

Heat the oil in a large wok and sauté the garlic and onion for 2 minutes or until light golden brown. Add the chicken and stir-fry for 3 minutes. Add the carrots, cabbage, oyster sauce, and pepper and stir-fry for 3 minutes, stirring occasionally. Add the green onions and egg noodles and stir-fry for 2 minutes, stirring frequently. Garnish with the coriander leaves.

Serves 4-6.

SEAFOOD CHOW MEIN

2 tablespoons canola oil
3 cloves garlic, crushed
1 small yellow onion,
  chopped
1 lb. large shrimp, shelled,
  deveined (see diagram,
  page 145)
1 large carrot, peeled, cut
  into julienne strips
1 lb. bean sprouts, washed,
  drained
1/4 cup fish sauce
4 green onions, cut into
  1-inch lengths
1 lb. cooked egg noodles
1/4 cup fresh coriander
  leaves, chopped

Heat the oil in a large wok and sauté the garlic and onion for 2 minutes or until light golden brown. Add the shrimp and carrot and stir-fry for 3 minutes, stirring frequently. Add the bean sprouts, fish sauce, green onions and egg noodles and stir-fry for 2 minutes or until well-mixed. Garnish with the coriander leaves.

Serves 4-6.

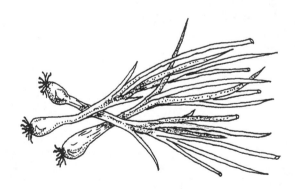

STIR-FRIED VERMICELLI

1 pkg. rice vermicelli (8 oz.)
3 tablespoons canola oil
3 cloves garlic, crushed
1 small yellow onion,
   chopped
1 lb. pork loin, thinly sliced
1/2 cup dried shrimp, soaked
   in 1/4 cup of warm water
   for 5 minutes (reserve the
   water)
2 large carrots, peeled, cut
   into julienne strips
12 snow pea pods, ends
   removed, cut into
   julienne strips
1/2 teaspoon ground white
   pepper
1/4 cup fish sauce
3 green onions, chopped
1/4 cup fresh coriander
   leaves, chopped

In a bowl with warm water, soak the rice vermicelli for 15 minutes and drain well. Set aside. Heat the oil in a large wok and sauté the garlic and onion for 2 minutes or until light golden brown. Add the pork and stir-fry for 3 minutes, stirring frequently. Add the shrimp with soaking water and carrots and stir-fry for 2 minutes. Add the vermicelli, pea pods, pepper, fish sauce and green onions and stir-fry for 3 more minutes, stirring occasionally. Garnish with the coriander leaves.

Serves 4-6.

CHAPTER NINE

DESSERTS

CHAPTER NINE

Desserts

Banana Tapioca Pudding

1 cup white sugar
2 cups water
4 whole ripe plantain
   bananas, peeled, cut
   diagonally into 2-inch
   strips
1/4 cup tapioca pearls,
   soaked in a 1/2 cup cold
   water, drained
1 can coconut milk
   (14 fl. oz.)
1/8 teaspoon salt

Bring the sugar, water, and bananas to a boil in a large pot over high heat for 2 minutes. Reduce the heat to low and cook covered for 15 minutes. Add the tapioca pearls and cook uncovered for 5 minutes, stirring occasionally, or until pearls are clear and translucent. Add the coconut milk and salt. Simmer for 2 minutes. Serve at room temperature or cold.

Serves 4-6.

Coconut Cookies

1 1/2 cups fine coconut
   flakes, unsweetened
2 egg whites
1/2 cup sugar
1/2 cup white flour, sifted
1/2 stick butter, melted

Brown the coconut flakes in a dry wok over moderate heat, stirring frequently to keep them from burning and to allow them to develop a uniform, deep golden color (approximately 5 minutes). Set aside. In a large bowl, beat the egg whites until foamy. Add the sugar and beat for 3 more minutes. Fold in the flour, butter, and toasted coconut flakes. Drop tablespoonsful of the cookie batter on a buttered cookie sheet, about 2 inches apart. Bake in a 350 degree oven for 15 to 20 minutes.

Makes 24 cookies.

Coconut Ice Cream

1 pint whipping cream
1 can coconut milk
  (14 fl. oz.)
1/8 teaspoon salt
1 cup white sugar

In a large bowl, mix the whipping cream, coconut milk, salt, and sugar. Put the mixture in an ice cream maker or place the mixture in a pan in the freezer and freeze it until it is icy and almost set. Scrape it into a mixing bowl and beat it thoroughly with a wooden spoon, or at low speed with an electric mixer. Return it to the freezer and freeze it until it is set.

Serves 4.

Jackfruit Ice Cream

1 can jackfruit in syrup
  (20 oz.)
1 pint whipping cream
1 teaspoon fresh, grated
  lime peel

Drain the jackfruit. Reserve the syrup. Chop the jackfruit very finely with a knife or food processor. In a large bowl, mix the syrup, chopped jackfruit, whipping cream, and grated lime peel. Put the mixture in an ice cream maker or place the mixture in a pan in the freezer and freeze it until it is icy and almost set. Scrape it into a mixing bowl and beat it thoroughly with a wooden spoon, or at low speed with an electric mixer. Return it to the freezer and freeze it until it is set.

Serves 4.

Mango Ice Cream

2 large ripe mangoes,
  peeled, seeded
1 cup white sugar
1/8 teaspoon salt
1 pint whipping cream
2 tablespoons fresh
  orange juice
1 large ripe mango, peeled,
  seeded, thinly sliced for
  decoration

In a blender, blend the mangoes, sugar, and salt. In a large bowl, mix the mango mixture with the whipping cream and orange juice. Put the mixture in an ice cream maker or place the mixture in a pan in the freezer and freeze it until it is icy and almost set. Scrape it into a mixing bowl and beat it thoroughly with a wooden spoon, or at low speed with an electric mixer. Return it to the freezer and freeze it until it is set. Serve with sliced mango on top.

Serves 4.

Sweet Potato Pudding

4 cups water
2 cups cubed sweet potatoes
1/4 cup tapioca sticks
1/8 teaspoon salt
1 cup sugar
1 can coconut milk
  (14 fl. oz.)

In a large pot, bring the water and sweet potatoes to a boil. Reduce the heat to low and simmer for 20 minutes or until the sweet potatoes are soft. Add the tapioca sticks, salt, and sugar and simmer for 10 minutes. Add the coconut milk and bring it to a simmer for 1 minute. Serve warm or at room temperature.

Serves 4-6.

VIETNAMESE CUSTARD

1/2 cup sugar for caramel
3 eggs, well-beaten
1 can sweetened condensed
  milk (12 fl. oz.)
1 cup milk
1 teaspoon vanilla

In a small heavy pan, melt the sugar over a low temperature until it is caramelized. Pour it into small individual heat-proof cups, tilting the cups so that the caramel coats the sides well. In a bowl, thoroughly mix the eggs, condensed milk, milk and vanilla. Pour it into the cups (about 1/2 cup of the mixture in each one) with the caramelized sugar. Steam in a large steamer over medium-high heat for 40 minutes or until the custards are set. Cool and unmold on individual small plates. Serve cold.

Serves 4-6.

YELLOW MUNG BEAN ICE CREAM

2 cups cooked yellow mung
  beans, mashed
1 pint whipping cream
1/2 cup milk
1 can coconut milk
  (14 fl. oz.)
1/8 teaspoon salt
1 cup white sugar

In a large bowl, mix the mashed mung beans, whipping cream, milk, coconut milk, salt and sugar. Put the mixture in an ice cream maker or place the mixture in a pan in the freezer and freeze it until it is icy and almost set. Scrape it into a mixing bowl and beat it thoroughly with a wooden spoon, or at low speed with an electric mixer. Return it to the freezer and freeze it until it is set.

Serves 4-6.

VIETNAMESE COFFEE

1/4 cup ground coffee
4 cups water
1 can sweetened, condensed
milk (12 fl. oz.)

Place 1½ tablespoons of sweetened condensed milk into a cup. Place 1 tablespoon of ground coffee into a 2 ½ inch Vietnamese coffee strainer. Place the strainer on the cup. Bring the water to a boil and pour 1 cup of boiling water over the ground coffee. Cover and wait a few seconds until the coffee drips into the cup. Remove the strainer and stir well. Repeat with each cup. Serve hot.

Serves 4.

VIETNAMESE ICED COFFEE

1/2 cup ground coffee
5 cups water
crushed ice
1 can sweetened, condensed
milk (12 fl. oz.)

Place a coffee filter in a 6-inch strainer and put the coffee into the filter and place it over a 2 quart pot. Bring the water to a boil and pour it over the coffee. Stir the water continuously in the coffee filter. Let it cool to lukewarm. Pour it into tall glasses filled with crushed ice. Add about 1 inch of condensed milk and stir well. Serve cold.

Serves 4-6.

VIETNAMESE MUNG BEAN PUDDING

4 cups water
1 pkg. yellow mung beans
(14. oz.), washed, drained
1 cup sugar
1 can coconut milk
(14 fl. oz.)

Bring the water and mung beans to a boil over high heat in a large, deep, uncovered pot for 2 minutes. Reduce the heat to low and simmer covered for 30 minutes or until the mung beans are soft. Add the sugar and coconut milk and simmer for 5 minutes. Serve warm.

Serves 4-6.

Cleaning and Scoring Squid

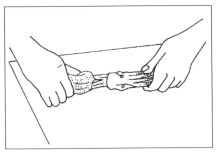

1. Pull the tentacles from the body of the squid; the intestines will also come out.

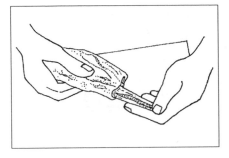

2. Pull out the quill from the body.

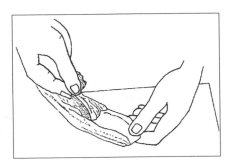

3. Peel off the outer skin, rinse out the body and cut the tentacles off at the head.

4. Cut to size, depending on the recipe.

Filling and Wrapping Wontons

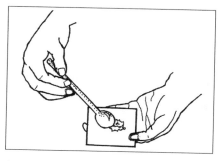

1. Place one teaspoonful of the pork mixture in the center of the wrapper.

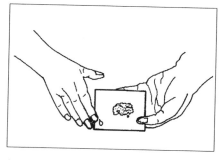

2. Wet the edges of the wrapper.

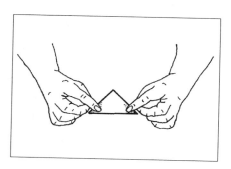

3. Fold it up into a triangle by pinching the three corners together.

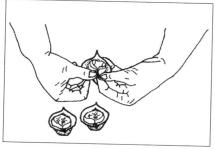

4. Wet one of the bottom corners of the triangle and fold it over to overlap the opposite corner and join them by pinching them together.

Shelling and Deveining Shrimp

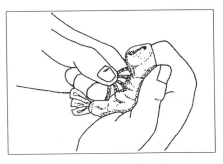

1. From the underside of shrimp, remove the legs.

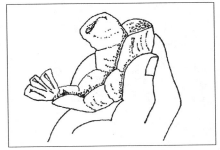

2. Roll back the shell from the underside, removing or keeping the tail, as desired.

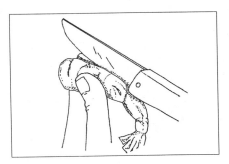

3. To devein, cut along the back (not completely through) and remove the vein.

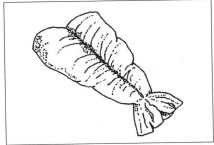

4. If butterflying is desired, cut deeper along the back and spread the halves open along the cut in the back.

Wrapping Spring Rolls

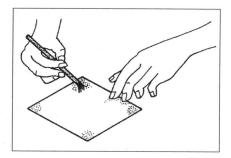

1. Place a wrapper with one corner toward you, and brush on a little egg yolk and water on each corner to seal the spring roll.

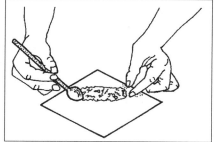

2. Put two tablespoons of the filling 1/3 of the way from the corner.

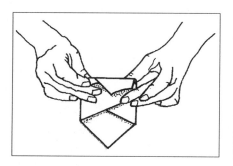

3. Fold the closest edge over the filling; then fold the right and left edges.

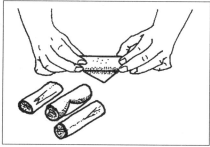

4. Roll up the spring roll, making sure the final edge sticks to the body.

Suggested Menus

A typical Vietnamese meal is an array of many different and exotic dishes presented together. Rice is the staple of every meal and tea is usually drunk while savoring the lovely combination of dishes. Below are listed combinations of three menu suggestions which can be enjoyed by you, your family and guests. Try them and enjoy.

Quick and Easy Menus

White Icicle Radish Salad, page 60
Vietnamese Barbecued Chicken, page 34
Savory Fish Sauce, page 18

Shrimp Salad, page 57
Hoisin Sauce, page 16
Vietnamese Barbecued Pork, page 34

Mixed Vegetable Pickles, page 13
Dried Shrimp with Tofu, page 92
Spicy Chicken with Mint Leaves, page 30

Kohlrabi Salad, page 55
Asparagus and Crab Meat Soup, page 37
Stuffed Tomatoes with Pork, page 74

Ground Pork and Taro Soup, page 41
Tofu with Eggplant, page 77
Stir-Fried Beef with Bamboo Shoots, page 104

Clams with Basil, page 83
Spicy Ground Chicken, page 123
Shrimp with Garlic, page 94

Vegetarian Menus

Soy Lime Sauce, page 19
Barbecued Tofu with Vegetables, page 23
Cauliflower with Baby Corn, page 64

Curried Mock Chicken, page 65
Mixed Vegetables with Lemon Grass, page 68
Tomatoes Stuffed with Tofu, page 79

Corn and Tofu Sour Soup, page 40
Vegetarian Spring Rolls, page 33
Mixed Vegetables with Tofu, page 69

Jicama with Tofu Salad, page 54
Tofu Curry, page 75
Steamed Tofu with Green Onion, page 72

Carrot with Tofu Salad, page 53
Mixed Vegetable Soup, page 42
Tofu with Black Bean Sauce, page 76

Vegetable Tofu Soup, page 47
Tofu Corn Fritters, page 32
Vegetable Tofu Curry, page 80

Carrot Salad, page 52
Lemon Grass Mock Chicken, page 67
Long-Grain White Rice, page 129

Carrot and Cucumber Salad, page 52
Green Beans with Tofu, page 66
Black Mushrooms with Tofu, page 63

Cucumber Soup, page 40
White Icicle Radish Pickles, page 14
Cauliflower with Mushrooms, page 64

Elegant Menus

Chicken and Crab Meat Soup, page 37
Lime Sauce, page 16
Sweet and Sour Sauce, page 19
Beef Lemon Grass Satay, page 24
Beef Salad with Vegetables, page 51
Stuffed Baked Fish, page 91
Banana Tapioca Pudding, page 137

Sweet and Sour Soup, page 45
Deep-Fried Wontons, page 25
Sweet and Spicy Sauce, page 20
Pork and Shrimp Vegetable Salad, page 56
Shrimp Curry, page 93
Coconut Ice Cream, page 138

Chicken with Lily Bud Soup, page 39
Ground Shrimp on Bread, page 26
Savory Fish Sauce, page 18
Spicy Chicken Salad, page 58
Fried Fish in Tomato Sauce, page 88
Jackfruit Ice Cream, page 138

Corn and Crab Meat Soup, page 39
Fish Curry with Lemon Grass, page 86
Spicy Fried Tofu, page 70
Shrimp with Snow Peas, page 95
Stuffed Squid with Pork, page 98
Mango Ice Cream, page 139

Savory Clams, page 83
Shrimp Sour Soup, page 44
Tomatoes Stuffed with Crab, page 78
Fried Sweet and Sour Sauce, page 89
Shrimp with Vegetables, page 96
Stir-Fried Beef with Broccoli, page 105
Vietnamese Custard, page 140

Essential Ingredients

Bay Laurel Leaves
Canned Bamboo Shoots
Canned Braised Gluten
Canned Coconut Milk
Canned Coconut Soda
Canned Water Chestnuts
*Canola Oil
Cayenne Peppers
Cellophane Noodles
Curry Powder
Dried Black Chinese Mushrooms
Dried Black Fungus
Dried Plums
Dried Rice Papers
Dried Shrimp
Dried Shrimp Paste or Sauce
Fish Sauce
Five Spice Powder
Flat Rice Stick Noodles
Fresh Coriander Leaves
Fresh Mint Leaves
Fresh or Canned Jackfruit
Fresh or Frozen Gluten
Frozen Pork Skin
Ginger
Hoisin Sauce

Holy or Sweet Basil Leaves
Japanese Eggplant
Jicama
Kohlrabi
Lemon Grass
Light Soy Sauce
Lily Buds
Maggi Seasoning Sauce
Oyster Sauce
Plantain Banana
Rice Vermicelli
Rice Vinegar
Roasted Peanuts
Salted Chinese Black Beans
Sesame Oil
Sesame Seeds
Shallots
Soy Bean Paste
Staranise
Tapioca Pearls
Tapioca Sticks
Taro root
Tofu
White Glutinous rice
White Icicle Radish Pickles
Yellow Mung Beans

*Any kind of oil may be used; however, for better cooking results and for health concerns, I use and recommend the following: for deep-frying, use a refined, high oleic, monounsaturated safflower oil (Spectrum Naturals) or canola oil; for stir-frying, use unrefined, high oleic, monounsaturated safflower oil (Spectrum Naturals) or canola oil. Safflower oil is available in health food stores; canola oil is readily available in supermarkets. In Vietnam, peanut oil, corn oil, soya oil, cottonseed oil, sesame oil and palm oil are usually used.

Glossary

BABY CORN: Miniature ears of corn, available in cans in Asian markets.

BAMBOO SHOOTS: A crisp, cream-colored, conical-shaped vegetable used frequently in all Asian cooking. It is much simpler to buy the canned variety which is readily available in all Asian and many Western markets.

BASIL: A strong pungent herb of which there are various types. The one type most often used in Vietnamese cooking is holy basil with a purple stem and a very distinctive flavor. Available in Asian and Western markets.

BLACK CHINESE MUSHROOMS: Although sold dried, they must be soaked in warm water for some time before using. The hard stems are discarded. Available in Asian and Western markets.

BLACK FUNGUS STRIPS: (Wood Fungus) Dried, they look like black strips of paper; however, they must be soaked in warm water for 10 minutes before using. They are bland with a crunchy texture, having little taste of their own, but taking on the flavor of whatever they are cooked with. Available in Asian markets.

BRAISED GLUTEN: Usually canned, but occasionally found fresh. When fresh, it is light brown and is made from enriched wheat flour, water, safflower oil, soy bean extract, sugar and salt. It is high in protein and has a chewy, meat-like texture. Available in Asian markets.

CAYENNE PEPPERS: Very hot peppers, available fresh or dried in most markets.

CELLOPHANE NOODLES: Also known as "bean thread vermicelli", a firm transparent noodle made from mung beans. They are usually soaked in warm water for 5 minutes before use. They are also deep-fried straight from the packet when used as a garnish.

CHINESE FIVE SPICE POWDER: It is a combination of ground star anise, licorice root, cinnamon, cloves, fennel, and ground black pepper. It is a very strong seasoning and should be used sparingly. Available in most markets.

COCONUT MILK: Made by combining freshly grated coconut with water, then squeezing and straining. Available in cans or powdered in most markets. No substitute.

COCONUT SODA: Also known as coconut flavored soda, it is a soft drink made from coconut extract. Available in Asian markets.

DRIED RICE PAPERS: Thin white rice papers made from rice, water, and salt. Sold dried in plastic packets. Available in Asian markets.

DRIED SHRIMP PASTE OR SAUCE: A strong pungent paste made from shrimp, and used in many Southeast Asian recipes. It is sold in cans, jars or flat slabs and will keep indefinitely. Available in Asian markets.

FISH SAUCE: A thin, salty, brown sauce used in Southeast Asian cooking to bring out the flavor in food. Available in Asian and Western markets.

FLAT RICE STICK NOODLES: White, flat noodles made from rice flour. Available in Asian markets.

FRESH CORIANDER: Also known as cilantro and Chinese parsley, it has a very distinctive flavor. It is available in seed form or ground. Available in most markets. No substitute.

FRESH MINT: There are many varieties; however, the common round-leafed mint (Spearmint) is the one most often used.

GINGER: A smooth-skinned, buff-colored root, used both for seasoning dishes and as a condiment.

GLUTINOUS RICE: A long-grained variety of rice known as sticky-rice or sweet rice. It is used frequently for rice desserts. Available in Asian markets.

HOISIN SAUCE: A sweet, reddish-brown thick sauce made from soy bean paste, garlic, sugar, and spices. Available in Asian markets.

HOLY BASIL: The variety of basil most often used in Vietnamese cooking, it has a purple stem and a strong pungent flavor. Sweet basil is a substitute.

JACK FRUIT: A yellow, strong-flavored fruit native to East India and Southeast Asia. Usually canned, but occasionally found fresh when in season. Available in Asian markets.

JAPANESE EGGPLANT: Four to six inches long and about two inches in diameter, this eggplant is very tasty and tender. Available in Asian and Western markets.

JICAMA: Usually thought of as a Mexican vegetable, jicama is a tuber common in Southeast Asia as well. Its availability and character make it a great substitute for fresh water chestnuts. It must be peeled before being used in a recipe. It has a sweet flavor and crunchy texture. Available in most markets.

KOHLRABI: A light green, turnip-like bulb with a mild flavor and crunchy texture. It is good raw or cooked. Available in most markets.

LEMON GRASS: An aromatic type of grass with a strong lemony fragrance, also known as "serah," it grows with a small bulbous root. Grated lemon peel can be used as a poor substitute. It is sold fresh, powdered, chopped, or in dried slices in Asian markets.

LILY BUDS: Very nutritious, long, narrow, dried golden buds with a very delicate flavor, they must be soaked in warm water for 20 minutes prior to use. Discard the hard stem ends and tie each bud in a knot, especially for soups. Available in Asian markets.

OYSTER SAUCE: Made from oysters cooked in salted water and soy sauce. It keeps well and adds a delicate flavor to meat and vegetable dishes.

PLANTAIN BANANA: A flattish, squarish, stubby banana which remains greenish-yellow even when ripe. It is the best of all the cooking bananas, especially for desserts.

RICE VERMICELLI: Thin, white noodles made from rice flour. Available in most markets.

SALTED BLACK BEANS: A highly flavorful ingredient made from black soy beans which have been cooked and fermented. Used to season meat, chicken and seafood. Available in Asian stores in cans or plastic bags.

SESAME OIL: Extracted from toasted sesame seeds, it is widely used in Oriental cooking in small quantities for flavoring. Available in Asian and Western markets.

SESAME SEEDS: Small flat seeds used as a source of oil and as a garnish. Available in Asian and Western markets.

SHALLOTS: Small, purplish sweet onions with red-brown skin. Available in Asian markets.

SOY BEAN PASTE: (Miso) A paste of fermented soy beans, cereal grain and sea salt. Available in Asian markets and in the gourmet food sections of supermarkets.

SPRING ROLL WRAPPERS: Thin white wrappers made from flour, water, and salt. Sold in plastic packets and kept frozen. Thaw and peel off one at a time (unused wrappers can be re-frozen). Available in Asian markets.

STAR ANISE: Dried, star-shaped spice of an evergreen tree native to China, it has a licorice flavor and should be stored in a tightly sealed jar. Available in Asian markets.

TAPIOCA PEARLS: Very tiny circles shaped like small pearls, made from ground cassava root and used for desserts. Available in Asian markets.

TAPIOCA STICKS: A thin 2-inch stick, made from ground cassava root and used for desserts. Sometimes available in colored sticks in small 7 oz. packets. Sold in Asian markets.

TARO ROOT: A starchy root used like potato, it adds a soothing heartiness to soups and desserts. All are covered with a coarse, dark skin that must first be peeled off, and have creamy-colored flesh with reddish-brown specks. Peel and cut just before using, as taro root discolors quickly. Available in Asian markets.

TOFU: (Soy Bean Curd) A soft white curd which is made from soy beans and resembles fresh white cheese. It is bland, having little taste of its own, but taking on the flavor of whatever it is cooked with. It is high in protein and low in calories; it is low in saturated fat and is cholesterol-free. It is also rich in vitamins and minerals. Four kinds of Tofu are widely available (Soft, Medium, Firm, and Extra Firm) which are sold in little plastic containers that are transparent so that you can look through the top. Each container of tofu weighs 10 to 16 ounces. Available in Asian and Western markets.

WATER CHESTNUTS: Usually canned, but occasionally found fresh, water chestnuts have a crunchy texture. When fresh, their brown skin must be peeled off with a sharp knife and discarded.

WHITE ICICLE RADISH: (Daikon) A long white, sweet radish native to Japan, it is often served grated with deep-fried, oily foods, as it is considered an aid to digestion. Available in Asian and health food stores.

YELLOW MUNG BEANS: Green-skinned mung beans which have been peeled and dried. Available in Asian markets.

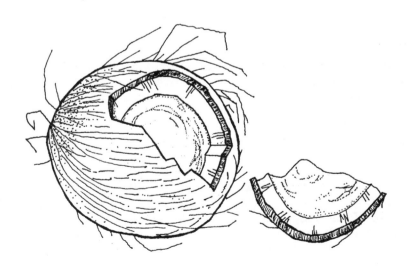

Index

Truly **Ambrosia**

Delightful Tofu Cooking

Delightful Vietnamese Cooking

Delightful Brazilian Cooking

Delightful Thai Cooking

coming soon

Delightful Chinese Cooking

Delightful Indonesian Cooking

Delightful Italian Cooking

Ordering Information

Please send me:

___copies of Delightful Tofu Cooking, $12.95 each $_____

___copies of Delightful Vietnamese Cooking, $12.95 each $_____

___copies of Delightful Brazilian Cooking, $14.95 each $_____

___copies of Delightful Thai Cooking, $10.95 each $_____

___set of 4 copies, $40.00 a set $_____

Shipping & Handling:

          $3.00   1st copy $_____

          $1.00   each additional copy $_____

          $6.00   set of 4 $_____

Washington State residents add 8.2% sales tax. $_____

                   Total Enclosed $_____

Payment:

❑ Check   ❑ Money Order

Mail Payment To:

Ambrosia Publications
P.O. Box 30818
Seattle, WA 98103
Phone (206) 789-3693
Fax (206) 789- 3693

Ship Order To:

Name _____

Address _____

City _____

State _____ Zip Code _____

❑Autographed by the author ? To whom ? _____